Just The facts101

Textbook Key Facts

e-Study Guide

by cram101

Textbook NOT Included

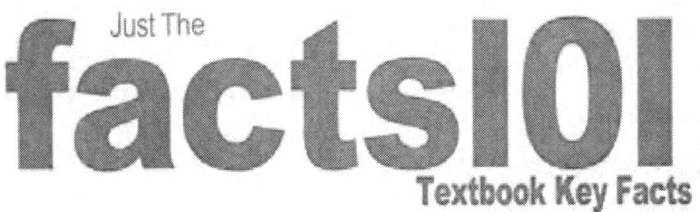

Textbook Outlines, Highlights, and Practice Quizzes

Water Chemistry

by Snoeyink & Jenkins, 1st Edition

All "Just the Facts101" Material Written or Prepared by Cram101 Publishing

Title Page

WHY STOP HERE... THERE'S MORE ONLINE

With technology and experience, we've developed tools that make studying easier and efficient. Like this Cram101 textbook notebook, **Cram101.com** offers you the highlights from every chapter of your actual textbook. However, unlike this notebook, **Cram101.com** gives you practice tests for each of the chapters. You also get access to in-depth reference material for writing essays and papers.

By purchasing this book, you get 50% off the normal subscription free!. Just enter the promotional code **'DK73DW2184'** on the Cram101.com registration screen.

CRAM101.COM FEATURES:

Outlines & Highlights
Just like the ones in this notebook, but with links to additional information.

Integrated Note Taking
Add your class notes to the Cram101 notes, print them and maximize your study time.

Problem Solving
Step-by-step walk throughs for math, stats and other disciplines.

Practice Exams
Five different test taking formats for every chapter.

Easy Access
Study any of your books, on any computer, anywhere.

Unlimited Textbooks
All the features above for virtually all your textbooks, just add them to your account at no additional cost.

Be sure to use the promo code above when registering on Cram101.com to get 50% off your membership fees.

STUDYING MADE EASY

This Cram101 notebook is designed to make studying easier and increase your comprehension of the textbook material. Instead of starting with a blank notebook and trying to write down everything discussed in class lectures, you can use this Cram101 textbook notebook and annotate your notes along with the lecture.

Our goal is to give you the best tools for success.

For a supreme understanding of the course, pair your notebook with our online tools. Should you decide you prefer Cram101.com as your study tool,

we'd like to offer you a trade...

Our Trade In program is a simple way for us to keep our promise and provide you the best studying tools, regardless of where you purchased your Cram101 textbook notebook. As long as your notebook is in *Like New Condition**, you can send it back to us and we will immediately give you a Cram101.com account free for 120 days!

Let The *Trade In* Begin!

THREE SIMPLE STEPS TO TRADE:

1. Go to www.cram101.com/tradein and fill out the packing slip information.
2. Submit and print the packing slip and mail it in with your Cram101 textbook notebook.
3. Activate your account after you receive your email confirmation.

* Books must be returned in *Like New Condition*, meaning there is no damage to the book including, but not limited to; ripped or torn pages, markings or writing on pages, or folded / creased pages. Upon receiving the book, Cram101 will inspect it and reserves the right to terminate your free Cram101.com account and return your textbook notebook at the owners expense.

"Just the Facts101" is a Cram101 publication and tool designed to give you all the facts from your textbooks. Visit Cram101.com for the full practice test for each of your chapters for virtually any of your textbooks.

Cram101 has built custom study tools specific to your textbook. We provide all of the factual testable information and unlike traditional study guides, we will never send you back to your textbook for more information.

YOU WILL NEVER HAVE TO HIGHLIGHT A BOOK AGAIN!

Cram101 StudyGuides
All of the information in this StudyGuide is written specifically for your textbook. We include the key terms, places, people, and concepts... the information you can expect on your next exam!

Want to take a practice test?
Throughout each chapter of this StudyGuide you will find links to cram101.com where you can select specific chapters to take a complete test on, or you can subscribe and get practice tests for up to 12 of your textbooks, along with other exclusive cram101.com tools like problem solving labs and reference libraries.

Cram101.com
Only cram101.com gives you the outlines, highlights, and PRACTICE TESTS specific to your textbook. Cram101.com is an online application where you'll discover study tools designed to make the most of your limited study time.

By purchasing this book, you get 50% off the normal subscription free!. Just enter the promotional code **'DK73DW2184'** on the Cram101.com registration screen.

www.Cram101.com

Copyright © 2012 by Cram101, Inc. All rights reserved.
"Just the FACTS101"®, "Cram101"® and "Never Highlight a Book Again!"® are registered trademarks of Cram101, Inc.
ISBN(s): 9781428829985. PUBE-3.2012220

Learning System

Water Chemistry
Snoeyink & Jenkins, 1st

CONTENTS

1. ONE - INTRODUCTION 9
2. TWO - CHEMICAL KINETICS 27
3. THREE - CHEMICAL EQUILIBRIUM 41
4. FOUR - ACID-BASE CHEMISTRY 64
5. FIVE - COORDINATION CHEMISTRY 82
6. SIX - PRECIPITATION AND DISSOLUTION 102
7. SEVEN - OXIDATION - REDUCTION REACTIONS 137

CHAPTER OUTLINE: KEY TERMS, PEOPLE, PLACES, CONCEPTS
Chapter 1
ONE - INTRODUCTION

- Phenanthroline
- Phenol
- Nitrogen trichloride
- Hydrogen
- Seawater
- Cadmium
- Solubility
- Atmosphere
- Earth
- Groundwater
- Surface water
- Gas constant
- Agriculture
- Wastewater
- Catalysis
- Concentration
- Activity
- Activity coefficient
- Solution

Chapter 1. ONE - INTRODUCTION

- Biochemical oxygen demand
- Chemical oxygen demand
- Oxygen
- Hardness

CHAPTER HIGHLIGHTS: KEY TERMS, PEOPLE, PLACES, CONCEPTS
Chapter 1. ONE - INTRODUCTION

Phenanthroline	Phenanthroline is a heterocyclic organic compound. As a bidentate ligand in coordination chemistry, it forms strong complexes with most metal ions. In terms of its coordination properties, phen is similar to 2,2'-bipyridine (bipy).
Phenol	Phenol is an organic compound with the chemical formula C_6H_5OH. It is a white crystalline solid. The molecule consists of a phenyl ($-C_6H_5$), bonded to a hydroxyl (-OH) group. It is produced on a large scale (about 7 billion kg/year) as a precursor to many materials and useful compounds. It is only mildly acidic but requires careful handling due to its propensity to cause burns.
Nitrogen trichloride	Nitrogen trichloride, trichlorine nitride (incorrect in nomenclature of binary compounds; Nitrogen trichloride is a sound name following the rules of systematic nomenclature) is the chemical compound with the formula NCl_3. This yellow, oily, pungent-smelling liquid is most commonly encountered as a byproduct of chemical reactions between ammonia-derivatives and chlorine (for example, in swimming pools between disinfecting chlorine and urea in urine from bathers). In pure form, NCl_3 is highly reactive.
Hydrogen	Hydrogen is the chemical element with atomic number 1. It is represented by the symbol H. With an average atomic weight of 1.007 94 u (1.007 825 u for Hydrogen-1), hydrogen is the lightest and most abundant chemical element, constituting roughly 75 % of the Universe's chemical elemental mass. Stars in the main sequence are mainly composed of hydrogen in its plasma state. Naturally occurring elemental hydrogen is relatively rare on Earth.
Seawater	Seawater is water from a sea or ocean. On average, seawater in the world's oceans has a salinity of about 3.5% (35 g/L, or 599 mM). This means that every kilogram (roughly one litre by volume) of seawater has approximately 35 grams (1.2 oz) of dissolved salts (predominantly Sodium Chloride ions: Na^+, Cl^-).
Cadmium	Cadmium is a chemical element with the symbol Cd and atomic number 48. The soft, bluish-white metal is chemically similar to the two other metals in group 12, zinc and mercury. Similar to zinc it prefers oxidation state +2 in most of its compounds and similar to mercury it shows a low melting point compared to transition metals. Cadmium and its congeners are not considered transition metals, in that they do not have partly filled d or f electron shells in the elemental or common oxidation states.

Chapter 1. ONE - INTRODUCTION

Solubility	Solubility is the property of a solid, liquid, or gaseous chemical substance called solute to dissolve in a liquid solvent to form a homogeneous solution of the solute in the solvent. The solubility of a substance fundamentally depends on the used solvent as well as on temperature and pressure. The extent of the solubility of a substance in a specific solvent is measured as the saturation concentration where adding more solute does not increase the concentration of the solution.
Atmosphere	An atmosphere is a layer of gases that may surround a material body of sufficient mass, and that is held in place by the gravity of the body. An atmosphere may be retained for a longer duration, if the gravity is high and the atmosphere's temperature is low. Some planets consist mainly of various gases, but only their outer layer is their atmosphere.
Earth	The chemical term earths was historically applied to certain chemical substances, once thought to be elements, and this name was borrowed from one of the four classical elements of Plato. 'Earths' later turned out to be chemical compounds, albeit difficult to concentrate, such as rare earths and alkaline earths. Actually, earths are metallic oxides, and the corresponding metals were classified into the corresponding groups: rare earth metals and alkaline earth metals.
Groundwater	Groundwater is water located beneath the ground surface in soil pore spaces and in the fractures of rock formations. A unit of rock or an unconsolidated deposit is called an aquifer when it can yield a usable quantity of water. The depth at which soil pore spaces or fractures and voids in rock become completely saturated with water is called the water table.
Surface water	Surface water is water collecting on the ground or in a stream, river, lake, wetland, or ocean; it is related to water collecting as groundwater or atmospheric water. Surface water is naturally replenished by precipitation and naturally lost through discharge to evaporation and sub-surface seepage into the groundwater. Although there are other sources of groundwater, such as connate water and magmatic water, precipitation is the major one and groundwater originated in this way is called meteoric water.

Chapter 1. ONE - INTRODUCTION

Gas constant	The gas constant is a physical constant which is featured in a large number of fundamental equations in the physical sciences, such as the ideal gas law and the Nernst equation. It is equivalent to the Boltzmann constant, but expressed in units of energy (i.e. the pressure-volume product) per kelvin per mole (rather than energy per kelvin per particle). Its value is $$R = 8.314472(15) \ \frac{J}{mol \ K}$$ The two digits in parentheses are the uncertainty (standard deviation) in the last two digits of the value.
Agriculture	Agriculture is the cultivation of animals, plants, fungi and other life forms for food, fiber, and other products used to sustain life. Agriculture was the key implement in the rise of sedentary human civilization, whereby farming of domesticated species created food surpluses that nurtured the development of civilization. The study of agriculture is known as agricultural science.
Wastewater	Wastewater is any water that has been adversely affected in quality by anthropogenic influence. It comprises liquid waste discharged by domestic residences, commercial properties, industry, and/or agriculture and can encompass a wide range of potential contaminants and concentrations. In the most common usage, it refers to the municipal wastewater that contains a broad spectrum of contaminants resulting from the mixing of wastewaters from different sources.
Catalysis	Catalysis is the change in rate of a chemical reaction due to the participation of a substance called a catalyst. Unlike other reagents that participate in the chemical reaction, a catalyst is not consumed by the reaction itself. A catalyst may participate in multiple chemical transformations.
Concentration	In chemistry, concentration is defined as the abundance of a constituent divided by the total volume of a mixture. Furthermore, in chemistry, four types of mathematical description can be distinguished: mass concentration, molar concentration, number concentration, and volume concentration. The term concentration can be applied to any kind of chemical mixture, but most frequently it refers to solutes in solutions.

Chapter 1. ONE - INTRODUCTION

Activity	In chemical thermodynamics, activity is a measure of the 'effective concentration' of a species in a mixture. By convention, it is treated as a dimensionless quantity, although its actual value depends on customary choices of standard state for the species. The activity of pure substances in condensed phases (solid or liquids) is normally taken as unity.
Activity coefficient	An activity coefficient is a factor used in thermodynamics to account for deviations from ideal behaviour in a mixture of chemical substances. In an ideal mixture, the interactions between each pair of chemical species are the same (or more formally, the enthalpy of mixing is zero) and, as a result, properties of the mixtures can be expressed directly in terms of simple concentrations or partial pressures of the substances present e.g. Raoult's law. Deviations from ideality are accommodated by modifying the concentration by an activity coefficient.
Solution	In chemistry, a solution is a homogeneous mixture composed of two or more substances. In such a mixture, a solute is dissolved in another substance, known as a solvent. The solvent does the dissolving.
Biochemical oxygen demand	Biochemical oxygen demand or B.O.D. is the amount of dissolved oxygen needed by aerobic biological organisms in a body of water to break down organic material present in a given water sample at certain temperature over a specific time period. The term also refers to a chemical procedure for determining this amount. This is not a precise quantitative test, although it is widely used as an indication of the organic quality of water.
Chemical oxygen demand	In environmental chemistry, the chemical oxygen demand test is commonly used to indirectly measure the amount of organic compounds in water. Most applications of Chemical oxygen demand determine the amount of organic pollutants found in surface water (e.g. lakes and rivers), making Chemical oxygen demand a useful measure of water quality. It is expressed in milligrams per liter (mg/L), which indicates the mass of oxygen consumed per liter of solution.
Oxygen	Oxygen is the element with atomic number 8 and represented by the symbol O. At standard temperature and pressure, two atoms of the element bind to form dioxygen, a colorless, odorless, tasteless diatomic gas with the formula O_2. Oxygen is a member of the chalcogen group on the periodic table, and is a highly reactive nonmetallic element that readily forms compounds (notably oxides) with almost all other elements. By mass, oxygen is the third most abundant element in the universe after hydrogen and helium and the most abundant element by mass in the Earth's crust, making up almost half of the crust's mass.

Chapter 1. ONE - INTRODUCTION

Hardness

Hardness is the measure of how resistant solid matter is to various kinds of permanent shape change when a force is applied. Macroscopic hardness is generally characterized by strong intermolecular bonds, however the behavior of solid materials under force is complex, therefore there are different measurements of hardness: scratch hardness, indentation hardness, and rebound hardness.

Hardness is dependent on ductility, elasticity, plasticity, strain, strength, toughness, viscoelasticity, and viscosity.

PRACTICE QUIZ
Chapter 1. ONE - INTRODUCTION

1. _____ is a heterocyclic organic compound. As a bidentate ligand in coordination chemistry, it forms strong complexes with most metal ions. In terms of its coordination properties, phen is similar to 2,2'-bipyridine (bipy).

    a. Resazurin
    b. Phenanthroline
    c. Tetrazolium chloride
    d. 1,2-Dioxetane

2. _____ is an organic compound with the chemical formula C_6H_5OH. It is a white crystalline solid. The molecule consists of a phenyl ($-C_6H_5$), bonded to a hydroxyl (-OH) group. It is produced on a large scale (about 7 billion kg/year) as a precursor to many materials and useful compounds. It is only mildly acidic but requires careful handling due to its propensity to cause burns.

    a. 1,2-Dioxetane
    b. Safranin
    c. Tetrazolium chloride
    d. Phenol

3. _____ is water located beneath the ground surface in soil pore spaces and in the fractures of rock formations. A unit of rock or an unconsolidated deposit is called an aquifer when it can yield a usable quantity of water. The depth at which soil pore spaces or fractures and voids in rock become completely saturated with water is called the water table.

    a. Hydraulic head
    b. 1,2-Dioxetane
    c. 1,3,5-Trioxane
    d. Groundwater

4. _____ is the change in rate of a chemical reaction due to the participation of a substance called a catalyst. Unlike other reagents that participate in the chemical reaction, a catalyst is not consumed by the reaction itself. A catalyst may participate in multiple chemical transformations.

    a. Catalysis
    b. Kinetic capillary electrophoresis
    c. Phase-boundary catalysis
    d. Reaction progress kinetic analysis

5. _____ is water from a sea or ocean. On average, _____ in the world's oceans has a salinity of about 3.5% (35 g/L, or 599 mM). This means that every kilogram (roughly one litre by volume) of _____ has approximately 35 grams (1.2 oz) of dissolved salts (predominantly Sodium Chloride ions: Na^+, Cl^-).

----

a. 1,2-Dioxetane
b. Nickel
c. Selenium
d. Seawater

ANSWER KEY
Chapter 1. ONE - INTRODUCTION

1. b
2. d
3. d
4. a
5. d

You can take the complete Chapter Practice Test

for Chapter 1. ONE - INTRODUCTION
on all key terms, persons, places, and concepts.

Online 99 Cents

http://www.epub14.6.2184.1.cram101.com/

Use www.Cram101.com for all your study needs

including Cram101's online interactive problem solving labs in chemistry, statistics, mathematics, and more.

CHAPTER OUTLINE: KEY TERMS, PEOPLE, PLACES, CONCEPTS
Chapter 2
TWO - CHEMICAL KINETICS

- Chemical kinetics
- Sulfide
- Redox
- Solubility
- Atmosphere
- Calcium
- Earth
- Hydroxylapatite
- Oxide
- Precipitation
- Orientation
- Silver chloride
- Chloride
- Sodium
- Sodium acetate
- Acetate
- Hydrogen
- Hydrogen peroxide
- Peroxide

Chapter 2. TWO - CHEMICAL KINETICS

- Cyclopropane
- Elementary reaction
- Radioactive decay
- Reaction mechanism
- Hydrogen bromide
- Hydrogen iodide
- Iodine
- Nitrogen
- Nitrogen dioxide
- Bromide
- Iodide
- Enzyme
- Enzyme kinetics
- Fructose
- Glucose
- Hydrolysis
- Activated complex
- Activation
- Activation energy

Chapter 2. TWO - CHEMICAL KINETICS

- Catalyst
- Enthalpy
- Detergent
- Pyrophosphoric acid
- Oxygen
- Pyrophosphate
- Sodium sulfite
- Sulfite
- Cyanate
- Cyanide
- Carbonization
- Carbon
- Activated sludge
- Sludge
- Biochemical oxygen demand
- Chemical oxygen demand

CHAPTER HIGHLIGHTS: KEY TERMS, PEOPLE, PLACES, CONCEPTS
Chapter 2. TWO - CHEMICAL KINETICS

Chemical kinetics	Chemical kinetics, is the study of rates of chemical processes. Chemical kinetics includes investigations of how different experimental conditions can influence the speed of a chemical reaction and yield information about the reaction's mechanism and transition states, as well as the construction of mathematical models that can describe the characteristics of a chemical reaction. In 1864, Peter Waage and Cato Guldberg pioneered the development of chemical kinetics by formulating the law of mass action, which states that the speed of a chemical reaction is proportional to the quantity of the reacting substances.
Sulfide	A sulfide is an anion of sulfur in its lowest oxidation state of 2-. Sulfide is also a slightly archaic term for thioethers, a common type of organosulfur compound that are well known for their bad odors. Properties The dianion S^{2-} exists only in strongly alkaline aqueous solutions.
Redox	Redox reactions describe all chemical reactions in which atoms have their oxidation number (oxidation state) changed. This can be either a simple redox process, such as the oxidation of carbon to yield carbon dioxide (CO_2) or the reduction of carbon by hydrogen to yield methane (CH_4), or a complex process such as the oxidation of sugar ($C_6H_{12}O_6$) in the human body through a series of complex electron transfer processes. The term comes from the two concepts of reduction and oxidation.
Solubility	Solubility is the property of a solid, liquid, or gaseous chemical substance called solute to dissolve in a liquid solvent to form a homogeneous solution of the solute in the solvent. The solubility of a substance fundamentally depends on the used solvent as well as on temperature and pressure. The extent of the solubility of a substance in a specific solvent is measured as the saturation concentration where adding more solute does not increase the concentration of the solution.
Atmosphere	An atmosphere is a layer of gases that may surround a material body of sufficient mass, and that is held in place by the gravity of the body. An atmosphere may be retained for a longer duration, if the gravity is high and the atmosphere's temperature is low. Some planets consist mainly of various gases, but only their outer layer is their atmosphere.

Chapter 2. TWO - CHEMICAL KINETICS

Calcium	Calcium is the chemical element with the symbol Ca and atomic number 20. It has an atomic mass of 40.078 amu. Calcium is a soft gray alkaline earth metal, and is the fifth most abundant element by mass in the Earth's crust. Calcium is also the fifth most abundant dissolved ion in seawater by both molarity and mass, after sodium, chloride, magnesium, and sulfate.
Earth	The chemical term earths was historically applied to certain chemical substances, once thought to be elements, and this name was borrowed from one of the four classical elements of Plato. 'Earths' later turned out to be chemical compounds, albeit difficult to concentrate, such as rare earths and alkaline earths. Actually, earths are metallic oxides, and the corresponding metals were classified into the corresponding groups: rare earth metals and alkaline earth metals.
Hydroxylapatite	Hydroxylapatite, is a naturally occurring mineral form of calcium apatite with the formula $Ca_5(PO_4)_3(OH)$, but is usually written $Ca_{10}(PO_4)_6(OH)_2$ to denote that the crystal unit cell comprises two entities. Hydroxylapatite is the hydroxyl endmember of the complex apatite group. The OH⁻ ion can be replaced by fluoride, chloride or carbonate, producing fluorapatite or chlorapatite.
Oxide	An oxide is an anion of oxygen in the oxidation state of −2 or a chemical compound formally containing an oxygen in this state. Most of the Earth's crust consists of oxides. Oxides result when elements are oxidized by oxygen in air.
Precipitation	Precipitation is the formation of a solid in a solution or inside another solid during a chemical reaction or by diffusion in a solid. When the reaction occurs in a liquid, the solid formed is called the precipitate, or when compacted by a centrifuge, a pellet. The liquid remaining above the solid is in either case called the supernate or supernatant.
Orientation	In mathematics, orientation is a notion that in two dimensions allows one to say when a cycle goes around clockwise or counterclockwise, and in three dimensions when a figure is left-handed or right-handed. In linear algebra, the notion of orientation makes sense in arbitrary dimensions. In this setting, the orientation of an ordered basis is a kind of asymmetry that makes a reflection impossible to replicate by means of a simple rotation.

Chapter 2. TWO - CHEMICAL KINETICS

Silver chloride	Silver chloride is a chemical compound with the chemical formula AgCl. This white crystalline solid is well known for its low solubility in water (this behavior being reminiscent of the chlorides of Tl^+ and Pb^{2+}). Upon illumination or heating, silver chloride converts to silver (and chlorine), which is signalled by greyish or purplish coloration to some samples.
Chloride	The chloride ion is formed when the element chlorine picks up one electron to form an anion (negatively-charged ion) Cl^-. The salts of hydrochloric acid HCl contain chloride ions and can also be called chlorides. Terminology The word chloride can also refer to a chemical compound in which one or more chlorine atoms are covalently bonded in the molecule.
Sodium	Sodium is a metallic element with a symbol Na and atomic number 11. It is a soft, silvery-white, highly reactive metal and is a member of the alkali metals within 'group 1' (formerly known as 'group IA'). It has only one stable isotope, ^{23}Na. Elemental sodium was first isolated by Humphry Davy in 1807 by passing an electric current through molten sodium hydroxide.
Sodium acetate	Sodium acetate, $NaC_2H_3O_2$, also sodium ethanoate, is the sodium salt of acetic acid. This colourless salt has a wide range of uses. Applications Industrial Sodium acetate is used in the textile industry to neutralize sulfuric acid waste streams, and as a photoresist while using aniline dyes.

Chapter 2. TWO - CHEMICAL KINETICS

Acetate	An acetate is a derivative of acetic acid. This term includes salts and esters, as well as the anion found in solution. Most of the approximately 5 billion kilograms of acetic acid produced annually in industry are used in the production of acetates, which usually take the form of polymers. In nature, acetate is the most common building block for biosynthesis. For example, the fatty acids are produced by connecting C2 units derived from acetate.
Hydrogen	Hydrogen is the chemical element with atomic number 1. It is represented by the symbol H. With an average atomic weight of 1.007 94 u (1.007 825 u for Hydrogen-1), hydrogen is the lightest and most abundant chemical element, constituting roughly 75 % of the Universe's chemical elemental mass. Stars in the main sequence are mainly composed of hydrogen in its plasma state. Naturally occurring elemental hydrogen is relatively rare on Earth.
Hydrogen peroxide	Hydrogen peroxide is an oxidizer commonly used as a bleach. It is the simplest peroxide (a compound with an oxygen-oxygen single bond). Hydrogen peroxide is a clear liquid, slightly more viscous than water, that appears colorless in dilute solution.
Peroxide	A peroxide is a compound containing an oxygen-oxygen single bond or the peroxide anion ([O–O]$^{2-}$). The O–O group is called the peroxide group or peroxo group. In contrast to oxide ions, the oxygen atoms in the peroxide ion have an oxidation state of −1.
Cyclopropane	Cyclopropane is a cycloalkane molecule with the molecular formula C_3H_6, consisting of three carbon atoms linked to each other to form a ring, with each carbon atom bearing two hydrogen atoms. Cyclopropane and propene have the same empirical formula but have different structures, making them structural isomers. The bonds between the carbon atoms are considerably weaker than in a typical carbon-carbon bond, yielding reactivity similar to or greater than alkenes.
Elementary reaction	An elementary reaction is a chemical reaction in which one or more of the chemical species react directly to form products in a single reaction step and with a single transition state.

Chapter 2. TWO - CHEMICAL KINETICS

In a unimolecular elementary reaction a molecule, A, dissociates or isomerises to form the products(s).

$$A \rightarrow products$$

The rate of such a reaction, at constant temperature, is proportional to the concentration of the species A

$$\frac{d[A]}{dt} = -k[A]$$

In a bimolecular elementary reaction, two atoms, molecules, ions or radicals, A and B, react together to form the product(s)

$$A + B \rightarrow products$$

The rate of such a reaction, at constant temperature, is proportional to the product of the concentrations of the species A and B.

$$\frac{d[A]}{dt} = \frac{d[B]}{dt} = -k[A][B]$$

This rate expression can be derived from first principles by using collision theory.

Radioactive decay

Radioactive decay is the process by which an atomic nucleus of an unstable atom loses energy by emitting ionizing particles (ionizing radiation). The emission is spontaneous, in that the atom decays without any interaction with another particle from outside the atom (i.e., without a nuclear reaction). Usually, radioactive decay happens due to a process confined to the nucleus of the unstable atom, but, on occasion (as with the different processes of electron capture and internal conversion), an inner electron of the radioactive atom is also necessary to the process.

Chapter 2. TWO - CHEMICAL KINETICS

Reaction mechanism	In chemistry, a reaction mechanism is the step by step sequence of elementary reactions by which overall chemical change occurs.
	Although only the net chemical change is directly observable for most chemical reactions, experiments can often be designed that suggest the possible sequence of steps in a reaction mechanism. Recently, electrospray ionization mass spectrometry has been used to corroborate the mechanism of several organic reaction proposals.
Hydrogen bromide	Hydrogen bromide is the diatomic molecule Hydrogen bromider. Hydrogen bromider is a gas at standard conditions. Hydrobromic acid forms upon dissolving Hydrogen bromider in water.
Hydrogen iodide	Hydrogen iodide is a diatomic molecule. Aqueous solutions of Hydrogen iodide are known as iohydroic acid or hydroiodic acid, a strong acid. Gas and aqueous solution are interconvertible.
Iodine	Iodine is a chemical element that has the symbol I and the atomic number 53.
	Iodine and its compounds are primarily used in nutrition, the production of acetic acid and polymers. Iodine's relatively high atomic number, low toxicity, and ease of attachment to organic compounds have made it a part of many X-ray contrast materials in modern medicine.
Nitrogen	Nitrogen is a chemical element that has the symbol N, atomic number of 7 and atomic mass 14.00674 u. Elemental nitrogen is a colorless, odorless, tasteless and mostly inert diatomic gas at standard conditions, constituting 78.08% by volume of Earth's atmosphere. The element nitrogen was discovered as a separable component of air, by Scottish physician Daniel Rutherford, in 1772.
Nitrogen dioxide	Nitrogen dioxide is the chemical compound with the formula NO_2. One of several nitrogen oxides, NO_2 is an intermediate in the industrial synthesis of nitric acid, millions of tons of which are produced each year. This reddish-brown toxic gas has a characteristic sharp, biting odor and is a prominent air pollutant.
Bromide	

Chapter 2. TWO - CHEMICAL KINETICS

A bromide is a chemical compound containing bromide ion, that is bromine atom with effective charge of −1. The class name can include ionic compounds such as caesium bromide or covalent compounds such as sulfur dibromide.

Natural occurrence

Bromide is present in typical seawater (35 PSU) with a concentration of around 65 mg/L, which is around 0.2% of all dissolved salts. Seafoods generally have high levels of bromide, while foods derived from land have variable amounts.

Iodide	An iodide ion is the ion I^-. Compounds with iodine in formal oxidation state −1 are called iodides. This page is for the iodide ion and its salts.
Enzyme	Enzymes are proteins that catalyze (i.e., increase or decrease the rates of) chemical reactions. In enzymatic reactions, the molecules at the beginning of the process are called substrates, and they are converted into different molecules, called the products. Almost all processes in a biological cell need enzymes to occur at significant rates.
Enzyme kinetics	Enzyme kinetics is the study of the chemical reactions that are catalysed by enzymes. In enzyme kinetics, the reaction rate is measured and the effects of varying the conditions of the reaction investigated. Studying an enzyme's kinetics in this way can reveal the catalytic mechanism of this enzyme, its role in metabolism, how its activity is controlled, and how a drug or a poison might inhibit the enzyme.
Fructose	Fructose, is a simple monosaccharide found in many foods. It is one of the three important dietary monosaccharides along with glucose and galactose. The organic fructose molecule was first discovered by Augustin-Pierre Dubrunfaut in 1847. Fructose is a white solid that dissolves in water - it is the most water-soluble of all the sugars.
Glucose	Glucose is a simple sugar (monosaccharide) and an important carbohydrate in biology. Cells use it as the primary source of energy and a metabolic intermediate. Glucose is one of the main products of photosynthesis and starts cellular respiration.

Chapter 2. TWO - CHEMICAL KINETICS

Hydrolysis	Hydrolysis is a chemical reaction during which molecules of water (H_2O) are split into hydrogen cations (H^+, conventionally referred to as protons) and hydroxide anions (OH^-) in the process of a chemical mechanism. It is the type of reaction that is used to break down certain polymers, especially those made by condensation polymerization. Such polymer degradation is usually catalysed by either acid, e.g., concentrated sulfuric acid (H_2SO_4), or alkali, e.g., sodium hydroxide (NaOH).
Activated complex	In chemistry an activated complex is defined by the International Union of Pure and Applied Chemistry as 'that assembly of atoms which corresponds to an arbitrary infinitesimally small region at or near the col (saddle point) of a potential energy surface'. In other words, it refers to a collection of intermediate structures in a chemical reaction that persist while bonds are breaking and new bonds are forming. It therefore represents not one defined state, but rather a range of transient configurations that a collection of atoms passes through in between clearly defined products and reactants.
Activation	Activation in (bio-)chemical sciences generally refers to the process whereby something is prepared or excited for a subsequent reaction. Chemistry In chemistry, activation of molecules is where the molecules enter a state that avails for a chemical reaction to occur. The phrase energy of activation refers to the energy the reactants must acquire before they can successfully react with each other to produce the products, that is, to reach the transition state.
Activation energy	In chemistry, activation energy is a term introduced in 1889 by the Swedish scientist Svante Arrhenius, that is defined as the energy that must be overcome in order for a chemical reaction to occur. Activation energy may also be defined as the minimum energy required to start a chemical reaction. The activation energy of a reaction is usually denoted by E_a, and given in units of kilojoules per mole.
Catalyst	Catalyst is a science centre and museum devoted to the chemical industry. Its full title is Catalyst Science Discovery Centre. It is located in Widnes, Cheshire, in the north west of England, and situated on the north bank of the River Mersey (grid reference SJ512841).

Chapter 2. TWO - CHEMICAL KINETICS

Enthalpy	Enthalpy is a measure of the total energy of a thermodynamic system. It includes the internal energy, which is the energy required to create a system, and the amount of energy required to make room for it by displacing its environment and establishing its volume and pressure. Enthalpy is a thermodynamic potential.
Detergent	A detergent is a surfactant or a mixture of surfactants having 'cleaning properties in dilute solutions.' Commonly, 'detergent' refers to alkylbenzenesulfonates, a family of compounds that are similar to soap but are less affected by hard water. In most household contexts, the term detergent by itself refers specifically to laundry detergent or dish detergent, vs hand soap or other types of cleaning agents. Detergents are commonly available as powders or concentrated solutions.
Pyrophosphoric acid	Pyrophosphoric acid, also known under the name diphosphoric acid, is colorless, odorless, hygroscopic and is soluble in water, diethyl ether, and ethyl alcohol. It is produced from phosphoric acid by dehydration. Pyrophosphoric acid slowly hydrolyzes in the presence of water into phosphoric acid.
Oxygen	Oxygen is the element with atomic number 8 and represented by the symbol O. At standard temperature and pressure, two atoms of the element bind to form dioxygen, a colorless, odorless, tasteless diatomic gas with the formula O_2. Oxygen is a member of the chalcogen group on the periodic table, and is a highly reactive nonmetallic element that readily forms compounds (notably oxides) with almost all other elements. By mass, oxygen is the third most abundant element in the universe after hydrogen and helium and the most abundant element by mass in the Earth's crust, making up almost half of the crust's mass.
Pyrophosphate	In chemistry, the anion, the salts, and the esters of pyrophosphoric acid are called pyrophosphates. Any salt or ester containing two phosphate groups is called a diphosphate. As a food additive, diphosphates are known as E450.

Chapter 2. TWO - CHEMICAL KINETICS

Sodium sulfite	Sodium sulfite is a soluble sodium salt of sulfurous acid. It is a product of sulfur dioxide scrubbing, a part of the flue gas desulfurization process. It is also used as a preservative to prevent dried fruit from discoloring, and for preserving meats, and is used in the same way as sodium thiosulfate to convert elemental halides to their respective acids, in photography and for reducing chlorine levels in pools.
Sulfite	Sulfites are compounds that contain the sulfite ion SO_2- 3. The sulfite ion is the conjugate base of bisulfite. Although the acid itself is elusive, its salts are widely used. The structure of the sulfite anion can be described with three equivalent resonance structures. In each resonance structure, the sulfur atom is double-bonded to one oxygen atom with a formal charge of zero (neutral), and sulfur is singly bonded to the other two oxygen atoms, which each carry a formal charge of −1, together accounting for the −2 charge on the anion.
Cyanate	The cyanate ion is an anion with the chemical formula written as $[OCN]^-$ or $[NCO]^-$. In aqueous solution it acts as a base, forming isocyanic acid, HNCO. The cyanate ion is an ambidentate ligand, forming complexes with a metal ion in which either the nitrogen or oxygen atom may be the electron-pair donor. It can also act as a bridging ligand.
Cyanide	A cyanide is a chemical compound that contains the cyano group, C≡N, which consists of a carbon atom triple-bonded to a nitrogen atom. Most commonly, cyanides refers to salts of the anion CN^-. Most cyanides are highly toxic.
Carbonization	Carbonization is the term for the conversion of an organic substance into carbon or a carbon-containing residue through pyrolysis or destructive distillation. It is often used in organic chemistry with reference to the generation of coal gas and coal tar from raw coal. Fossil fuels in general are the products of the carbonization of vegetable matter.
Carbon	Carbon is the chemical element with symbol C and atomic number 6. As a member of group 14 on the periodic table, it is nonmetallic and tetravalent--making four electrons available to form covalent chemical bonds. There are three naturally occurring isotopes, with ^{12}C and ^{13}C being stable, while ^{14}C is radioactive, decaying with a half-life of about 5730 years. Carbon is one of the few elements known since antiquity.
Activated sludge	Activated sludge is a process for treating sewage and industrial wastewaters using air and a biological floc composed of bacteria and protozoans. Purpose

Chapter 2. TWO - CHEMICAL KINETICS

In a sewage (or industrial wastewater) treatment plant, the activated sludge process can be used for one or several of the following purposes:

- oxidizing carbonaceous matter: biological matter.
- oxidizing nitrogenous matter: mainly ammonium and nitrogen in biological materials.
- removing phosphate.
- driving off entrained gases carbon dioxide, ammonia, nitrogen, etc.
- generating a biological floc that is easy to settle.
- generating a liquor that is low in dissolved or suspended material.

The process
The process involves air or oxygen being introduced into a mixture of primary treated or screened sewage or industrial wastewater (called wastewater from now on) combined with organisms to develop a biological floc which reduces the organic content of the sewage. This material, which in healthy sludge is a brown floc, is largely composed of saprotrophic bacteria but also has an important protozoan flora mainly composed of amoebae, Spirotrichs, Peritrichs including Vorticellids and a range of other filter feeding species.

Sludge	Sludge refers to the residual, semi-solid material left from industrial wastewater, or sewage treatment processes. It can also refer to the settled suspension obtained from conventional drinking water treatment, and numerous other industrial processes. The term is also sometimes used as a generic term for solids separated from suspension in a liquid; this 'soupy' material usually contains significant quantities of 'interstitial' water (between the solid particles).
Biochemical oxygen demand	Biochemical oxygen demand or B.O.D. is the amount of dissolved oxygen needed by aerobic biological organisms in a body of water to break down organic material present in a given water sample at certain temperature over a specific time period. The term also refers to a chemical procedure for determining this amount. This is not a precise quantitative test, although it is widely used as an indication of the organic quality of water.
Chemical oxygen demand	In environmental chemistry, the chemical oxygen demand test is commonly used to indirectly measure the amount of organic compounds in water. Most applications of Chemical oxygen demand determine the amount of organic pollutants found in surface water (e.g. lakes and rivers), making Chemical oxygen demand a useful measure of water quality. It is expressed in milligrams per liter (mg/L), which indicates the mass of oxygen consumed per liter of solution.

PRACTICE QUIZ
Chapter 2. TWO - CHEMICAL KINETICS

1. _____ is a process for treating sewage and industrial wastewaters using air and a biological floc composed of bacteria and protozoans.

   Purpose
   In a sewage (or industrial wastewater) treatment plant, the _____ process can be used for one or several of the following purposes:

   - oxidizing carbonaceous matter: biological matter.
   - oxidizing nitrogenous matter: mainly ammonium and nitrogen in biological materials.
   - removing phosphate.
   - driving off entrained gases carbon dioxide, ammonia, nitrogen, etc.
   - generating a biological floc that is easy to settle.
   - generating a liquor that is low in dissolved or suspended material.

   The process
   The process involves air or oxygen being introduced into a mixture of primary treated or screened sewage or industrial wastewater (called wastewater from now on) combined with organisms to develop a biological floc which reduces the organic content of the sewage. This material, which in healthy sludge is a brown floc, is largely composed of saprotrophic bacteria but also has an important protozoan flora mainly composed of amoebae, Spirotrichs, Peritrichs including Vorticellids and a range of other filter feeding species.

   a. Air dryer
   b. Air permeability specific surface
   c. Activated sludge
   d. Air preheater

2. _____, is the study of rates of chemical processes. _____ includes investigations of how different experimental conditions can influence the speed of a chemical reaction and yield information about the reaction's mechanism and transition states, as well as the construction of mathematical models that can describe the characteristics of a chemical reaction. In 1864, Peter Waage and Cato Guldberg pioneered the development of _____ by formulating the law of mass action, which states that the speed of a chemical reaction is proportional to the quantity of the reacting substances.

   a. Chemical kinetics
   b. Reactions on surfaces
   c. Receptor-ligand kinetics
   d. Catalysis

----

3. _____ in (bio-)chemical sciences generally refers to the process whereby something is prepared or excited for a subsequent reaction.

Chemistry

In chemistry, _____ of molecules is where the molecules enter a state that avails for a chemical reaction to occur. The phrase energy of _____ refers to the energy the reactants must acquire before they can successfully react with each other to produce the products, that is, to reach the transition state.

   a. Elasticity Coefficient
   b. Entropy of activation
   c. Induction period
   d. Activation

4. _____, is a naturally occurring mineral form of calcium apatite with the formula $Ca_5(PO_4)_3(OH)$, but is usually written $Ca_{10}(PO_4)_6(OH)_2$ to denote that the crystal unit cell comprises two entities. _____ is the hydroxyl endmember of the complex apatite group. The OH^- ion can be replaced by fluoride, chloride or carbonate, producing fluorapatite or chlorapatite.

   a. Pygg
   b. Quartz inversion
   c. Hydroxylapatite
   d. Titanium diboride

5. _____s are proteins that catalyze (i.e., increase or decrease the rates of) chemical reactions. In enzymatic reactions, the molecules at the beginning of the process are called substrates, and they are converted into different molecules, called the products. Almost all processes in a biological cell need _____s to occur at significant rates.

   a. Agmatine
   b. Enzyme inducer
   c. Enzyme
   d. Isomer

ANSWER KEY
Chapter 2. TWO - CHEMICAL KINETICS

1. c
2. a
3. d
4. c
5. c

You can take the complete Chapter Practice Test

for Chapter 2. TWO - CHEMICAL KINETICS

on all key terms, persons, places, and concepts.

Online 99 Cents

http://www.epub14.6.2184.2.cram101.com/

Use www.Cram101.com for all your study needs

including Cram101's online interactive problem solving labs in chemistry, statistics, mathematics, and more.

CHAPTER OUTLINE: KEY TERMS, PEOPLE, PLACES, CONCEPTS
Chapter 3
THREE - CHEMICAL EQUILIBRIUM

- Chemical equilibrium
- Nature
- Activity
- Chemical kinetics
- Equilibrium constant
- Amorphous carbon
- Enthalpy
- Calcite
- Calcium
- Calcium carbonate
- Dissolution
- Precipitation
- Activity coefficient
- Mole
- Mole fraction
- Partial pressure
- Reaction quotient
- Hydroxide
- Redox

Chapter 3. THREE - CHEMICAL EQUILIBRIUM

- Solubility
- Nitrate
- Sulfide
- Endothermic
- Exothermic
- Exothermic reaction
- Sulfuric acid
- Ionic strength
- Strength
- Conductivity
- Total dissolved solids
- Salting out
- Seawater
- Cadmium
- Oxygen
- Electrode

CHAPTER HIGHLIGHTS: KEY TERMS, PEOPLE, PLACES, CONCEPTS
Chapter 3. THREE - CHEMICAL EQUILIBRIUM

Chemical equilibrium	In a chemical reaction, chemical equilibrium is the state in which the concentrations of the reactants and products have not yet changed with time. It occurs only in reversible reactions, and not in irreversible reactions. Usually, this state results when the forward reaction proceeds at the same rate as the reverse reaction.
Nature	Nature, in the broadest sense, is equivalent to the natural world, physical world, or material world. 'Nature' refers to the phenomena of the physical world, and also to life in general. It ranges in scale from the subatomic to the cosmic.
Activity	In chemical thermodynamics, activity is a measure of the 'effective concentration' of a species in a mixture. By convention, it is treated as a dimensionless quantity, although its actual value depends on customary choices of standard state for the species. The activity of pure substances in condensed phases (solid or liquids) is normally taken as unity.
Chemical kinetics	Chemical kinetics, is the study of rates of chemical processes. Chemical kinetics includes investigations of how different experimental conditions can influence the speed of a chemical reaction and yield information about the reaction's mechanism and transition states, as well as the construction of mathematical models that can describe the characteristics of a chemical reaction. In 1864, Peter Waage and Cato Guldberg pioneered the development of chemical kinetics by formulating the law of mass action, which states that the speed of a chemical reaction is proportional to the quantity of the reacting substances.
Equilibrium constant	For a general chemical equilibrium $$\alpha A + \beta B ... \rightleftharpoons \sigma S + \tau T ...$$ the equilibrium constant can be defined by $$K = \frac{\{S\}^\sigma \{T\}^\tau ...}{\{A\}^\alpha \{B\}^\beta ...}$$ where {A} is the activity of the chemical species A, etc. (activity is a dimensionless quantity). It is conventional to put the activities of the products in the numerator and those of the reactants in the denominator.

Chapter 3. THREE - CHEMICAL EQUILIBRIUM

Amorphous carbon	Amorphous carbon, reactive carbon, is an allotrope of carbon that does not have any crystalline structure. As with all glassy materials, some short-range order can be observed. Amorphous carbon is often abbreviated to aC for general amorphous carbon, aC:H for hydrogenated amorphous carbon, or to ta-C for tetrahedral amorphous carbon.
Enthalpy	Enthalpy is a measure of the total energy of a thermodynamic system. It includes the internal energy, which is the energy required to create a system, and the amount of energy required to make room for it by displacing its environment and establishing its volume and pressure. Enthalpy is a thermodynamic potential.
Calcite	Calcite is a carbonate mineral and the most stable polymorph of calcium carbonate ($CaCO_3$). The other polymorphs are the minerals aragonite and vaterite. Aragonite will change to calcite at 470 ° C, and vaterite is even less stable.
Calcium	Calcium is the chemical element with the symbol Ca and atomic number 20. It has an atomic mass of 40.078 amu. Calcium is a soft gray alkaline earth metal, and is the fifth most abundant element by mass in the Earth's crust. Calcium is also the fifth most abundant dissolved ion in seawater by both molarity and mass, after sodium, chloride, magnesium, and sulfate.
Calcium carbonate	Calcium carbonate is a chemical compound with the formula $CaCO_3$. It is a common substance found in rocks in all parts of the world, and is the main component of shells of marine organisms, snails, pearls, and eggshells. Calcium carbonate is the active ingredient in agricultural lime, and is usually the principal cause of hard water.
Dissolution	Dissolution is the process by which a solid or liquid forms a solution in a solvent. In solids this can be explained as the breakdown of the crystal lattice into individual ions, atoms or molecules and their transport into the solvent. Dissolution testing is widely used in the pharmaceutical industry for optimization of formulation and quality control.
Precipitation	Precipitation is the formation of a solid in a solution or inside another solid during a chemical reaction or by diffusion in a solid. When the reaction occurs in a liquid, the solid formed is called the precipitate, or when compacted by a centrifuge, a pellet. The liquid remaining above the solid is in either case called the supernate or supernatant.

Chapter 3. THREE - CHEMICAL EQUILIBRIUM

Activity coefficient	An activity coefficient is a factor used in thermodynamics to account for deviations from ideal behaviour in a mixture of chemical substances. In an ideal mixture, the interactions between each pair of chemical species are the same (or more formally, the enthalpy of mixing is zero) and, as a result, properties of the mixtures can be expressed directly in terms of simple concentrations or partial pressures of the substances present e.g. Raoult's law. Deviations from ideality are accommodated by modifying the concentration by an activity coefficient.
Mole	The mole is a unit of measurement for the amount of substance or chemical amount. It is one of the base units in the International System of Units, and has the unit symbol mol.
	The name mole is an 1897 translation of the German unit Mol, coined by the chemist Wilhelm Ostwald in 1893, although the related concept of equivalent mass had been in use at least a century earlier.
Mole fraction	In chemistry, the mole fraction x_i is defined as the amount of a constituent n_i divided by the total amount of all constituents in a mixture n_{tot}: $$x_i = \frac{n_i}{n_{tot}}$$ The sum of all the mole fractions is equal to 1: $$\sum_{i=1}^{N} n_i = n_{tot}; \quad \sum_{i=1}^{N} x_i = 1$$ The mole fraction is also called the amount fraction. It is identical to the number fraction, which is defined as the number of molecules of a constituent N_i divided by the total number of all molecules N_{tot}. It is one way of expressing the composition of a mixture in a dimensionless size (mass fraction is another).

Chapter 3. THREE - CHEMICAL EQUILIBRIUM

Partial pressure	In a mixture of ideal gases, each gas has a partial pressure which is the pressure which the gas would have if it alone occupied the volume. The total pressure of a gas mixture is the sum of the partial pressures of each individual gas in the mixture. In chemistry, the partial pressure of a gas in a mixture of gases is defined as above.
Reaction quotient	In chemistry, a reaction quotient: Q_r is a function of the activities or concentrations of the chemical species involved in a chemical reaction. In the special case that the reaction is at equilibrium the reaction quotient is equal to the equilibrium constant. A general chemical reaction in which α moles of a reactant A and β moles of a reactant B react to give σ moles of a product S and τ moles of a product T can be written as αA + βB ⇌ σS + τT The reaction is written as an equilibrium even though in many cases it may appear to have gone to completion.
Hydroxide	The hydroxide ion is a diatomic anion with chemical formula OH^-. It consists of an oxygen and a hydrogen atom held together by a covalent bond, and carrying a negative electrical charge. It is a natural constituent of water.
Redox	Redox reactions describe all chemical reactions in which atoms have their oxidation number (oxidation state) changed. This can be either a simple redox process, such as the oxidation of carbon to yield carbon dioxide (CO_2) or the reduction of carbon by hydrogen to yield methane (CH_4), or a complex process such as the oxidation of sugar ($C_6H_{12}O_6$) in the human body through a series of complex electron transfer processes. The term comes from the two concepts of reduction and oxidation.

Chapter 3. THREE - CHEMICAL EQUILIBRIUM

Solubility	Solubility is the property of a solid, liquid, or gaseous chemical substance called solute to dissolve in a liquid solvent to form a homogeneous solution of the solute in the solvent. The solubility of a substance fundamentally depends on the used solvent as well as on temperature and pressure. The extent of the solubility of a substance in a specific solvent is measured as the saturation concentration where adding more solute does not increase the concentration of the solution.
Nitrate	The nitrate ion is a polyatomic ion with the molecular formula NO_3^- and a molecular mass of 62.0049 g/mol. Structure It is the conjugate base of nitric acid, consisting of one central nitrogen atom surrounded by three identically-bonded oxygen atoms in a trigonal planar arrangement. The nitrate ion carries a formal charge of -1. This results from a combination formal charge in which each of the three oxygens carries a $-2/3$ charge, whereas the nitrogen carries a +1 charge, all these adding up to formal charge of the polyatomic nitrate ion.
Sulfide	A sulfide is an anion of sulfur in its lowest oxidation state of 2-. Sulfide is also a slightly archaic term for thioethers, a common type of organosulfur compound that are well known for their bad odors. Properties The dianion S^{2-} exists only in strongly alkaline aqueous solutions.
Endothermic	In thermodynamics, the word endothermic describes a process or reaction in which the system absorbs energy from the surroundings in the form of heat. Its etymology stems from the Greek prefix endo-, meaning 'inside' and the Greek suffix -ther, meaning 'heat'. The opposite of an endothermic process is an exothermic process, one that releases energy in the form of heat.
Exothermic	In thermodynamics, the term exothermic describes a process or reaction that releases energy from the system, usually in the form of heat, but also in the form of light (e.g. a spark, flame, or explosion), electricity (e.g. a battery), or sound (e.g. burning hydrogen). Its etymology stems from the Greek prefix ex- (meaning 'outside') and the Greek word thermein (meaning 'to heat'). The term exothermic was first coined by Marcellin Berthelot.

Chapter 3. THREE - CHEMICAL EQUILIBRIUM

Exothermic reaction	An exothermic reaction is a chemical reaction that releases energy in the form of light or heat. It is the opposite of an endothermic reaction. Expressed in a chemical equation: reactants → products + energy Overview An exothermic reaction is a chemical reaction that is accompanied by the release of heat.
Sulfuric acid	Sulfuric acid is a strong mineral acid with the molecular formula H_2SO_4. Its historical name is vitriol. The salts of sulphuric acid are called sulfates.
Ionic strength	The ionic strength of a solution is a measure of the concentration of ions in that solution. Ionic compounds, when dissolved in water, dissociate into ions. The total electrolyte concentration in solution will affect important properties such as the dissociation or the solubility of different salts.
Strength	In explosive materials, strength is the parameter determining the ability of the explosive to move the surrounding material. It is related to the total gas yield of the reaction, and the amount of heat produced. Cf.
Conductivity	The conductivity of an electrolyte solution is a measure of its ability to conduct electricity. The SI unit of conductivity is siemens per meter (S/m). Conductivity measurements are used routinely in many industrial and environmental applications as a fast, inexpensive and reliable way of measuring the ionic content in a solution.

Chapter 3. THREE - CHEMICAL EQUILIBRIUM

Total dissolved solids	Total Dissolved Solids is a measure of the combined content of all inorganic and organic substances contained in a liquid in: molecular, ionized or micro-granular (colloidal sol) suspended form. Generally the operational definition is that the solids must be small enough to survive filtration through a sieve the size of two micrometer. Total dissolved solids are normally discussed only for freshwater systems, as salinity comprises some of the ions constituting the definition of Total dissolved solids. The principal application of Total dissolved solids is in the study of water quality for streams, rivers and lakes, although Total dissolved solids is not generally considered a primary pollutant (e.g. it is not deemed to be associated with health effects) it is used as an indication of aesthetic characteristics of drinking water and as an aggregate indicator of the presence of a broad array of chemical contaminants.
Salting out	Salting out is a method of separating proteins based on the principle that proteins are less soluble at high salt concentrations. The salt concentration needed for the protein to precipitate out of the solution differs from protein to protein. This process is also used to concentrate dilute solutions of proteins.
Seawater	Seawater is water from a sea or ocean. On average, seawater in the world's oceans has a salinity of about 3.5% (35 g/L, or 599 mM). This means that every kilogram (roughly one litre by volume) of seawater has approximately 35 grams (1.2 oz) of dissolved salts (predominantly Sodium Chloride ions: Na^+, Cl^-).
Cadmium	Cadmium is a chemical element with the symbol Cd and atomic number 48. The soft, bluish-white metal is chemically similar to the two other metals in group 12, zinc and mercury. Similar to zinc it prefers oxidation state +2 in most of its compounds and similar to mercury it shows a low melting point compared to transition metals. Cadmium and its congeners are not considered transition metals, in that they do not have partly filled d or f electron shells in the elemental or common oxidation states.
Oxygen	Oxygen is the element with atomic number 8 and represented by the symbol O. At standard temperature and pressure, two atoms of the element bind to form dioxygen, a colorless, odorless, tasteless diatomic gas with the formula O_2.
	Oxygen is a member of the chalcogen group on the periodic table, and is a highly reactive nonmetallic element that readily forms compounds (notably oxides) with almost all other elements. By mass, oxygen is the third most abundant element in the universe after hydrogen and helium and the most abundant element by mass in the Earth's crust, making up almost half of the crust's mass.

Chapter 3. THREE - CHEMICAL EQUILIBRIUM

Electrode	An electrode is an electrical conductor used to make contact with a nonmetallic part of a circuit (e.g. a semiconductor, an electrolyte or a vacuum). The word was coined by the scientist Michael Faraday from the Greek words elektron (meaning amber, from which the word electricity is derived) and hodos, a way.

PRACTICE QUIZ
Chapter 3. THREE - CHEMICAL EQUILIBRIUM

1. _____ is the formation of a solid in a solution or inside another solid during a chemical reaction or by diffusion in a solid. When the reaction occurs in a liquid, the solid formed is called the precipitate, or when compacted by a centrifuge, a pellet. The liquid remaining above the solid is in either case called the supernate or supernatant.

    a. Reactive flash volatilization
    b. Redistribution
    c. Precipitation
    d. Rescue fusion hybridization

2. For a general chemical equilibrium

$$\alpha A + \beta B ... \rightleftharpoons \sigma S + \tau T ...$$

   the _____ can be defined by

$$K = \frac{\{S\}^\sigma \{T\}^\tau ...}{\{A\}^\alpha \{B\}^\beta ...}$$

   where {A} is the activity of the chemical species A, etc. (activity is a dimensionless quantity). It is conventional to put the activities of the products in the numerator and those of the reactants in the denominator.

    a. Equilibrium unfolding
    b. ICE table
    c. Ion-association
    d. Equilibrium constant

3. _____, in the broadest sense, is equivalent to the natural world, physical world, or material world. '_____' refers to the phenomena of the physical world, and also to life in general. It ranges in scale from the subatomic to the cosmic.

    a. Nature
    b. Nonpoint source pollution
    c. Permaforestry
    d. Population equivalent

----

4. The _____ of a solution is a measure of the concentration of ions in that solution. Ionic compounds, when dissolved in water, dissociate into ions. The total electrolyte concentration in solution will affect important properties such as the dissociation or the solubility of different salts.

   a. Multiangle light scattering
   b. Ionic strength
   c. Coacervate
   d. Colloid-facilitated transport

5. _____ is a strong mineral acid with the molecular formula H_2SO_4. Its historical name is vitriol. The salts of sulphuric acid are called sulfates.

   a. 1,2-Dioxetane
   b. Enthalpy of neutralization
   c. Exergonic reaction
   d. Sulfuric acid

ANSWER KEY
Chapter 3. THREE - CHEMICAL EQUILIBRIUM

1. c
2. d
3. a
4. b
5. d

You can take the complete Chapter Practice Test

for Chapter 3. THREE - CHEMICAL EQUILIBRIUM
on all key terms, persons, places, and concepts.

Online 99 Cents

http://www.epub14.6.2184.3.cram101.com/

Use www.Cram101.com for all your study needs

including Cram101's online interactive problem solving labs in chemistry, statistics, mathematics, and more.

CHAPTER OUTLINE: KEY TERMS, PEOPLE, PLACES, CONCEPTS
Chapter 4
FOUR - ACID-BASE CHEMISTRY

_____ Proton

_____ Hydronium

_____ Ionization

_____ Amorphous carbon

_____ Solvent

_____ Product

_____ Strong acid

_____ Weak acid

_____ Weak base

_____ Equilibrium constant

_____ Nitric acid

_____ Solution

_____ Chemical kinetics

_____ Reaction rate

_____ Hydrogen

_____ Hydrogen sulfide

_____ Dissociation

_____ Sulfide

_____ Concentration

Chapter 4. FOUR - ACID-BASE CHEMISTRY

- Mass balance
- Phenanthroline
- Sodium chloride
- Bicarbonate
- Phosphoric acid
- Sodium
- Sodium bicarbonate
- Acid salt
- Hydrochloric acid
- Sodium hydroxide
- Hydroxide
- Ionic strength
- Strength
- Acetic acid
- Sodium hypochlorite
- Hypochlorite
- Hypochlorous acid
- Ammonia
- Sulfuric acid

Chapter 4. FOUR - ACID-BASE CHEMISTRY

- Ammonium
- Ammonium acetate
- Acetate
- Mixture
- Titration
- Titration curve
- Ion exchange
- Activated sludge
- Alum
- Flocculation
- Agriculture
- Chloride
- Sludge
- Calcium
- Calcium hydroxide
- Oxide
- Plating
- Precipitation
- Intensity

Chapter 4. FOUR - ACID-BASE CHEMISTRY

- Potassium
- Potassium chromate
- Biosynthesis
- Carbon
- Carbon dioxide
- Bromothymol blue
- Dry ice
- Closed system
- Alkalinity
- Methyl orange
- Carbonate alkalinity
- Phenol
- PH meter
- Mineral
- Chlorine

CHAPTER HIGHLIGHTS: KEY TERMS, PEOPLE, PLACES, CONCEPTS
Chapter 4. FOUR - ACID-BASE CHEMISTRY

Proton	The proton is a subatomic particle with an electric charge of +1 elementary charge. One or more protons are present in the nucleus of each atom, along with neutrons. The proton is also stable by itself and has a second identity as the hydrogen ion, H^+.
Hydronium	In chemistry, hydronium is the common name for the aqueous cation H_3O^+, the type of oxonium ion, produced by protonation of water. It is the positive ion present when an Arrhenius acid is dissolved in water, as Arrhenius acid molecules in solution give up a proton (a positive hydrogen ion, H^+) to the surrounding water molecules (H_2O). Determination of pH It is the presence of hydronium ion relative to hydroxide that determines a solution's pH. The molecules in pure water auto-dissociate into hydronium and hydroxide ions in the following equilibrium: $$2\ H_2O\ OH^- + H_3O^+$$ In pure water, there is an equal number of hydroxide and hydronium ions, so it has a neutral pH of 7. A pH value less than 7 indicates an acidic solution, and a pH value more than 7 indicates a basic solution.
Ionization	Ionization is the process of converting an atom or molecule into an ion by adding or removing charged particles such as electrons or other ions. This is often confused with dissociation. A substance may dissociate without necessarily producing ions.
Amorphous carbon	Amorphous carbon, reactive carbon, is an allotrope of carbon that does not have any crystalline structure. As with all glassy materials, some short-range order can be observed. Amorphous carbon is often abbreviated to aC for general amorphous carbon, aC:H for hydrogenated amorphous carbon, or to ta-C for tetrahedral amorphous carbon.

Chapter 4. FOUR - ACID-BASE CHEMISTRY

Solvent	A solvent is a liquid, solid, or gas that dissolves another solid, liquid, or gaseous solute, resulting in a solution that is soluble in a certain volume of solvent at a specified temperature. Common uses for organic solvents are in dry cleaning (e.g. tetrachloroethylene), as a paint thinner (e.g. toluene, turpentine), as nail polish removers and glue solvents (acetone, methyl acetate, ethyl acetate), in spot removers (e.g. hexane, petrol ether), in detergents (citrus terpenes), in perfumes (ethanol), and in chemical synthesis. The use of inorganic solvents (other than water) is typically limited to research chemistry and some technological processes.
Product	Product(s) are formed during chemical reactions as reagents are consumed. Products have lower energy than the reagents and are produced during the reaction according to the second law of thermodynamics. The released energy comes from changes in chemical bonds between atoms in reagent molecules and may be given off in the form of heat or light.
Strong acid	A strong acid is an acid that ionizes completely in an aqueous solution by losing one proton, according to the equation $$HA(aq) \rightarrow H^+(aq) + A^-(aq)$$ For sulfuric acid which is diprotic, the 'strong acid' designation refers only to dissociation of the first proton $$H_2SO_4(aq) \rightarrow H^+(aq) + HSO_4^-(aq)$$ More precisely, the acid must be stronger in aqueous solution than hydronium ion, so strong acids are acids with a $pK_a < -1.74$. An example is HCl for which $pK_a = -6.3$. This generally means that in aqueous solution at standard temperature and pressure, the concentration of hydronium ions is equal to the concentration of strong acid introduced to the solution. While strong acids are generally assumed to be the most corrosive, this is not always true. The carborane superacid H ($CHB_{11}Cl_{11}$), which is one million times stronger than sulfuric acid, is entirely non-corrosive, whereas the weak acid hydrofluoric acid (HF) is extremely corrosive and can dissolve, among other things, glass and all metals except iridium.
Weak acid	A weak acid is an acid that dissociates incompletely. It does not release all of its hydrogens in a solution, donating only a partial amount of its protons to the solution. These acids have higher pKa than strong acids, which release all of their hydrogen atoms when dissolved in water.

Chapter 4. FOUR - ACID-BASE CHEMISTRY

Weak base	In chemistry, a weak base is a chemical base that does not ionize fully in an aqueous solution. As Bronsted-Lowry bases are proton acceptors, a weak base may also be defined as a chemical base in which protonation is incomplete. This results in a relatively low pH level compared to strong bases.
Equilibrium constant	For a general chemical equilibrium $$\alpha A + \beta B ... \rightleftharpoons \sigma S + \tau T ...$$ the equilibrium constant can be defined by $$K = \frac{\{S\}^\sigma \{T\}^\tau ...}{\{A\}^\alpha \{B\}^\beta ...}$$ where {A} is the activity of the chemical species A, etc. (activity is a dimensionless quantity). It is conventional to put the activities of the products in the numerator and those of the reactants in the denominator.
Nitric acid	Nitric acid also known as aqua fortis and spirit of nitre, is a highly corrosive and toxic strong acid. Colorless when pure, older samples tend to acquire a yellow cast due to the accumulation of oxides of nitrogen. If the solution contains more than 86% nitric acid, it is referred to as fuming nitric acid.
Solution	In chemistry, a solution is a homogeneous mixture composed of two or more substances. In such a mixture, a solute is dissolved in another substance, known as a solvent. The solvent does the dissolving.

Chapter 4. FOUR - ACID-BASE CHEMISTRY

Chemical kinetics	Chemical kinetics, is the study of rates of chemical processes. Chemical kinetics includes investigations of how different experimental conditions can influence the speed of a chemical reaction and yield information about the reaction's mechanism and transition states, as well as the construction of mathematical models that can describe the characteristics of a chemical reaction. In 1864, Peter Waage and Cato Guldberg pioneered the development of chemical kinetics by formulating the law of mass action, which states that the speed of a chemical reaction is proportional to the quantity of the reacting substances.
Reaction rate	The reaction rate is intuitively defined as how fast or slow a reaction takes place. For example, the oxidation of iron under the atmosphere is a slow reaction which can take many years, but the combustion of butane in a fire is a reaction that takes place in fractions of a second. Chemical kinetics is the part of physical chemistry that studies reaction rates.
Hydrogen	Hydrogen is the chemical element with atomic number 1. It is represented by the symbol H. With an average atomic weight of 1.007 94 u (1.007 825 u for Hydrogen-1), hydrogen is the lightest and most abundant chemical element, constituting roughly 75 % of the Universe's chemical elemental mass. Stars in the main sequence are mainly composed of hydrogen in its plasma state. Naturally occurring elemental hydrogen is relatively rare on Earth.
Hydrogen sulfide	Hydrogen sulfide is the chemical compound with the formula H_2S. It is a colorless, very poisonous, flammable gas with the characteristic foul odor of rotten eggs at concentrations up to 100 parts per million. It often results from the bacterial breakdown of organic matter in the absence of oxygen, such as in swamps and sewers (anaerobic digestion). It also occurs in volcanic gases, natural gas, and some well waters.
Dissociation	Dissociation in chemistry and biochemistry is a general process in which ionic compounds (complexes, or salts) separate or split into smaller particles, ions, or radicals, usually in a reversible manner. When a Bronsted-Lowry acid is put in water, a covalent bond between an electronegative atom and a hydrogen atom is broken by heterolytic fission, which gives a proton and a negative ion. Dissociation is the opposite of association and recombination.
Sulfide	A sulfide is an anion of sulfur in its lowest oxidation state of 2-. Sulfide is also a slightly archaic term for thioethers, a common type of organosulfur compound that are well known for their bad odors. Properties

----

Chapter 4. FOUR - ACID-BASE CHEMISTRY

The dianion S^{2-} exists only in strongly alkaline aqueous solutions.

Concentration | In chemistry, concentration is defined as the abundance of a constituent divided by the total volume of a mixture. Furthermore, in chemistry, four types of mathematical description can be distinguished: mass concentration, molar concentration, number concentration, and volume concentration. The term concentration can be applied to any kind of chemical mixture, but most frequently it refers to solutes in solutions.

Mass balance | A mass balance is an application of conservation of mass to the analysis of physical systems. By accounting for material entering and leaving a system, mass flows can be identified which might have been unknown, or difficult to measure without this technique. The exact conservation law used in the analysis of the system depends on the context of the problem but all revolve around mass conservation, i.e. that matter cannot disappear or be created spontaneously.

Phenanthroline | Phenanthroline is a heterocyclic organic compound. As a bidentate ligand in coordination chemistry, it forms strong complexes with most metal ions. In terms of its coordination properties, phen is similar to 2,2'-bipyridine (bipy).

Sodium chloride | Sodium chloride, common salt, table salt, or halite, is an ionic compound with the formula NaCl. Sodium chloride is the salt most responsible for the salinity of the ocean and of the extracellular fluid of many multicellular organisms. As the major ingredient in edible salt, it is commonly used as a condiment and food preservative.

Bicarbonate | In inorganic chemistry, bicarbonate is an intermediate form in the deprotonation of carbonic acid. Its chemical formula is HCO_3^-.

Bicarbonate serves a crucial biochemical role in the physiological pH buffering system.

Phosphoric acid | Phosphoric acid, is a mineral (inorganic) acid having the chemical formula H_3PO_4. Orthophosphoric acid molecules can combine with themselves to form a variety of compounds which are also referred to as phosphoric acids, but in a more general way. The term phosphoric acid can also refer to a chemical or reagent consisting of phosphoric acids, usually orthophosphoric acid.

Chapter 4. FOUR - ACID-BASE CHEMISTRY

Sodium	Sodium is a metallic element with a symbol Na and atomic number 11. It is a soft, silvery-white, highly reactive metal and is a member of the alkali metals within 'group 1' (formerly known as 'group IA'). It has only one stable isotope, ^{23}Na. Elemental sodium was first isolated by Humphry Davy in 1807 by passing an electric current through molten sodium hydroxide.
Sodium bicarbonate	Sodium bicarbonate is the chemical compound with the formula $NaHCO_3$. Sodium bicarbonate is a white solid that is crystalline but often appears as a fine powder. It has a slightly salty, alkaline taste resembling that of washing soda (sodium carbonate).
Acid salt	Acid salt is a somewhat obscure term for a class of salts formed by the partial neutralization of diprotic or polyprotic acids. Because the parent acid is only partially neutralized, one or more replaceable hydrogen ions remain. Typical acid salts have one or more alkali (alkaline) metal ions as well as one or more protons.
Hydrochloric acid	Hydrochloric acid is a solution of hydrogen chloride (HCl) in water, that is a highly corrosive, strong mineral acid with many industrial uses. It is found naturally in gastric acid. Historically called muriatic acid or spirits of salt, hydrochloric acid was produced from vitriol (sulfuric acid) and common salt.
Sodium hydroxide	Sodium hydroxide also known as lye and caustic soda, is a caustic metallic base. It is used in many industries, mostly as a strong chemical base in the manufacture of pulp and paper, textiles, drinking water, soaps and detergents and as a drain cleaner. Worldwide production in 2004 was approximately 60 million tonnes, while demand was 51 million tonnes.
Hydroxide	The hydroxide ion is a diatomic anion with chemical formula OH^-. It consists of an oxygen and a hydrogen atom held together by a covalent bond, and carrying a negative electrical charge. It is a natural constituent of water.

Chapter 4. FOUR - ACID-BASE CHEMISTRY

Ionic strength	The ionic strength of a solution is a measure of the concentration of ions in that solution. Ionic compounds, when dissolved in water, dissociate into ions. The total electrolyte concentration in solution will affect important properties such as the dissociation or the solubility of different salts.
Strength	In explosive materials, strength is the parameter determining the ability of the explosive to move the surrounding material. It is related to the total gas yield of the reaction, and the amount of heat produced. Cf.
Acetic acid	Acetic acid, CH_3COOH is an organic acid that gives vinegar its sour taste and pungent smell. It is a weak acid, in that it is only a partially dissociated acid in an aqueous solution. Pure, water-free acetic acid is a colourless liquid that absorbs water from the environment (hygroscopy), and freezes at 16.5 °C (62 °F) to a colourless crystalline solid.
Sodium hypochlorite	Sodium hypochlorite is a chemical compound with the formula NaClO. Sodium hypochlorite solution, commonly known as bleach, is frequently used as a disinfectant or a bleaching agent. Production Hypochlorite was first produced in 1789 by Claude Louis Berthollet in his laboratory on the quay Javel in Paris, France, by passing chlorine gas through a solution of sodium carbonate. The resulting liquid, known as 'Eau de Javel' ('Javel water'), was a weak solution of sodium hypochlorite.
Hypochlorite	The hypochlorite ion, also known as chlorate(I) anion is ClO^-. A hypochlorite compound is a chemical compound containing this group, with chlorine in oxidation state +1. Hypochlorites are the salts of hypochlorous acid.
Hypochlorous acid	Hypochlorous acid is a weak acid with the chemical formula HClO. In the swimming pool industry, hypochlorous acid is referred to as HOCl. It forms when chlorine dissolves in water. HClO is an oxidizer, and in its sodium form Sodium hypochlorite, NaClO, or its calcium form Calcium hypochlorite, is used as a bleach, a deodorant, and a disinfectant.

Chapter 4. FOUR - ACID-BASE CHEMISTRY

Ammonia	Ammonia is a compound of nitrogen and hydrogen with the formula NH_3. It is a colourless gas with a characteristic pungent odour. Ammonia contributes significantly to the nutritional needs of terrestrial organisms by serving as a precursor to food and fertilizers.
Sulfuric acid	Sulfuric acid is a strong mineral acid with the molecular formula H_2SO_4. Its historical name is vitriol. The salts of sulphuric acid are called sulfates.
Ammonium	The ammonium cation is a positively charged polyatomic cation with the chemical formula NH_4^+. It is formed by the protonation of ammonia (NH_3). Ammonium is also a general name for positively charged or protonated substituted amines and quaternary ammonium cations (N^+R_4), where one or more hydrogen atoms are replaced by organic radical groups (indicated by R).
Ammonium acetate	Ammonium acetate is a chemical compound with the formula CH_3COONH_4 (or $C_2H_4O_2 \cdot NH_3$ or $C_2H_7NO_2$). It is a white solid, which can be derived from the reaction of ammonia and acetic acid. It is available commercially and, depending on grade, can be rather inexpensive.
Acetate	An acetate is a derivative of acetic acid. This term includes salts and esters, as well as the anion found in solution. Most of the approximately 5 billion kilograms of acetic acid produced annually in industry are used in the production of acetates, which usually take the form of polymers. In nature, acetate is the most common building block for biosynthesis. For example, the fatty acids are produced by connecting C2 units derived from acetate.
Mixture	In chemistry, a mixture is a material system made up by two or more different substances which are mixed together but are not combined chemically. Mixture refers to the physical combination of two or more substances the identities of which are retainedes are mixed in the form of alloys, solutions, suspensions, and colloids. Mixtures are the product of a mechanical blending or mixing of chemical substances like elements and compounds, without chemical bonding or other chemical change, so that each ingredient substance retains its own chemical properties and makeup.

Chapter 4. FOUR - ACID-BASE CHEMISTRY

Titration	Titration, is a common laboratory method of quantitative chemical analysis that is used to determine the unknown concentration of an identified analyte. Because volume measurements play a key role in titration, it is also known as volumetric analysis. A reagent, called the titrant or titrator is prepared as a standard solution.
Titration curve	Titrations are often recorded on titration curves, whose compositions are generally identical: the independent variable is the volume of the titrant, while the dependent variable is the pH of the solution (which changes depending on the composition of the two solutions). The equivalence point is a significant point on the graph (the point at which all of the starting solution, usually an acid, has been neutralized by the titrant, usually a base).
	It can be calculated precisely by finding the second derivative of the titration curve and computing the points of inflection (where the graph changes concavity); however, in most cases, simple visual inspection of the curve will suffice (in the curve given to the right, both equivalence points are visible, after roughly 15 and 30 mL of NaOH solution has been titrated into the oxalic acid solution.
Ion exchange	Ion exchange is an exchange of ions between two electrolytes or between an electrolyte solution and a complex. In most cases the term is used to denote the processes of purification, separation, and decontamination of aqueous and other ion-containing solutions with solid polymeric or mineralic 'ion exchangers'.
	Typical ion exchangers are ion exchange resins (functionalized porous or gel polymer), zeolites, montmorillonite, clay, and soil humus.
Activated sludge	Activated sludge is a process for treating sewage and industrial wastewaters using air and a biological floc composed of bacteria and protozoans.
	Purpose

Chapter 4. FOUR - ACID-BASE CHEMISTRY

In a sewage (or industrial wastewater) treatment plant, the activated sludge process can be used for one or several of the following purposes:

- oxidizing carbonaceous matter: biological matter.
- oxidizing nitrogenous matter: mainly ammonium and nitrogen in biological materials.
- removing phosphate.
- driving off entrained gases carbon dioxide, ammonia, nitrogen, etc.
- generating a biological floc that is easy to settle.
- generating a liquor that is low in dissolved or suspended material.

The process
The process involves air or oxygen being introduced into a mixture of primary treated or screened sewage or industrial wastewater (called wastewater from now on) combined with organisms to develop a biological floc which reduces the organic content of the sewage. This material, which in healthy sludge is a brown floc, is largely composed of saprotrophic bacteria but also has an important protozoan flora mainly composed of amoebae, Spirotrichs, Peritrichs including Vorticellids and a range of other filter feeding species.

Alum

Alum is both a specific chemical compound and a class of chemical compounds. The specific compound is the hydrated potassium aluminium sulfate (Potassium alum) with the formula $KAl(SO_4)_2 \cdot 12H_2O$. The wider class of compounds known as alums have the related empirical formula, $AB(SO_4)_2 \cdot 12H_2O$.

Uses

Industrial

Alums are useful for a range of industrial processes. They are soluble in water; have an astringent, acid, and sweetish taste; react acid to litmus; and crystallize in regular octahedra.

Flocculation

Flocculation, in the field of chemistry, is a process wherein colloids come out of suspension in the form of floc or flakes by the addition of a clarifying agent. The action differs from precipitation in that, prior to flocculation, colloids are merely suspended in a liquid and not actually dissolved in a solution. In the flocculated system, there is no formation of a cake, since all the flocs are in the suspension.

Chapter 4. FOUR - ACID-BASE CHEMISTRY

Agriculture	Agriculture is the cultivation of animals, plants, fungi and other life forms for food, fiber, and other products used to sustain life. Agriculture was the key implement in the rise of sedentary human civilization, whereby farming of domesticated species created food surpluses that nurtured the development of civilization. The study of agriculture is known as agricultural science.
Chloride	The chloride ion is formed when the element chlorine picks up one electron to form an anion (negatively-charged ion) Cl^-. The salts of hydrochloric acid HCl contain chloride ions and can also be called chlorides. Terminology The word chloride can also refer to a chemical compound in which one or more chlorine atoms are covalently bonded in the molecule.
Sludge	Sludge refers to the residual, semi-solid material left from industrial wastewater, or sewage treatment processes. It can also refer to the settled suspension obtained from conventional drinking water treatment, and numerous other industrial processes. The term is also sometimes used as a generic term for solids separated from suspension in a liquid; this 'soupy' material usually contains significant quantities of 'interstitial' water (between the solid particles).
Calcium	Calcium is the chemical element with the symbol Ca and atomic number 20. It has an atomic mass of 40.078 amu. Calcium is a soft gray alkaline earth metal, and is the fifth most abundant element by mass in the Earth's crust. Calcium is also the fifth most abundant dissolved ion in seawater by both molarity and mass, after sodium, chloride, magnesium, and sulfate.
Calcium hydroxide	Calcium hydroxide, traditionally called slaked lime, is an inorganic compound with the chemical formula $Ca(OH)_2$. It is a colourless crystal or white powder and is obtained when calcium oxide (called lime or quicklime) is mixed, or 'slaked' with water. It has many names including hydrated lime, builders lime, slack lime, cal, or pickling lime.
Oxide	An oxide is an anion of oxygen in the oxidation state of −2 or a chemical compound formally containing an oxygen in this state. Most of the Earth's crust consists of oxides. Oxides result when elements are oxidized by oxygen in air.

Chapter 4. FOUR - ACID-BASE CHEMISTRY

Plating	Plating is a surface covering in which a metal is deposited on a conductive surface. Plating has been done for hundreds of years, but it is also critical for modern technology. Plating is used to decorate objects, for corrosion inhibition, to improve solderability, to harden, to improve wearability, to reduce friction, to improve paint adhesion, to alter conductivity, for radiation shielding, and for other purposes.
Precipitation	Precipitation is the formation of a solid in a solution or inside another solid during a chemical reaction or by diffusion in a solid. When the reaction occurs in a liquid, the solid formed is called the precipitate, or when compacted by a centrifuge, a pellet. The liquid remaining above the solid is in either case called the supernate or supernatant.
Intensity	In physics, intensity is a measure of the energy flux, averaged over the period of the wave. The word 'intensity' here is not synonymous with 'strength', 'amplitude', or 'level', as it sometimes is in colloquial speech. For example, 'the intensity of pressure' is meaningless, since the parameters of those variables do not match.
Potassium	Potassium is the chemical element with the symbol K, atomic number 19, and atomic mass 39.0983. Elemental potassium is a soft silvery-white metallic alkali metal that oxidizes rapidly in air and is very reactive with water, generating sufficient heat to ignite the hydrogen emitted in the reaction. Potassium and sodium are alkali metals and are chemically very similar. For this reason, historically their salts were not differentiated.
Potassium chromate	Potassium chromate is a yellow chemical indicator used for identifying concentrations of chloride ions in a salt solution with silver nitrate ($AgNO_3$). It is a class two carcinogen and can cause cancer on inhalation. General information Physical properties Potassium Chromate is a lemon yellow compound that is in the form of a crystalline solid, and it is very stable.

Chapter 4. FOUR - ACID-BASE CHEMISTRY

Biosynthesis	Biosynthesis is an enzyme-catalyzed process in cells of living organisms by which substrates are converted to more complex products. The biosynthesis process often consists of several enzymatic steps in which the product of one step is used as substrate in the following step. Examples for such multi-step biosynthetic pathways are those for the production of amino acids, fatty acids, and natural products.
Carbon	Carbon is the chemical element with symbol C and atomic number 6. As a member of group 14 on the periodic table, it is nonmetallic and tetravalent--making four electrons available to form covalent chemical bonds. There are three naturally occurring isotopes, with ^{12}C and ^{13}C being stable, while ^{14}C is radioactive, decaying with a half-life of about 5730 years. Carbon is one of the few elements known since antiquity.
Carbon dioxide	Carbon dioxide is a chemical compound composed of two oxygen atoms covalently bonded to a single carbon atom. It is a gas at standard temperature and pressure and exists in Earth's atmosphere in this state. CO_2 is a trace gas comprising 0.039% of the atmosphere.
Bromothymol blue	Bromothymol blue is a chemical indicator for weak acids and bases. The chemical is also used for observing photosynthetic activities or respiratory indicators (turns yellow as CO_2 is added). Bromothymol blue acts as a weak acid in solution.
Dry ice	Dry ice is the solid form of carbon dioxide. Dry ice is used as a cooling agent. Moreover, for some applications, the convenience of its sublimation 'into thin air,' in contrast to the melt-water left by warming water ice, may outweigh other costs.
Closed system	The term closed system has different meanings in different contexts. In computing

----

Chapter 4. FOUR - ACID-BASE CHEMISTRY

	In computing a closed system refers to software which the specifications and detail of implementation (typically source code) are kept secret, as opposed to open source systems.
	In physics
	In thermodynamics, a closed system can exchange heat and work (for example, energy), but not matter, with its surroundings.
Alkalinity	Alkalinity or A_T measures the ability of a solution to neutralize acids to the equivalence point of carbonate or bicarbonate. The alkalinity is equal to the stoichiometric sum of the bases in solution. In the natural environment carbonate alkalinity tends to make up most of the total alkalinity due to the common occurrence and dissolution of carbonate rocks and presence of carbon dioxide in the atmosphere.
Methyl orange	Methyl orange is a pH indicator frequently used in titrations.
	It is often used in titrations because of its clear colour change. Because it changes colour at the pH of a mid-strength acid, it is usually used in titrations for acids.
Carbonate alkalinity	Carbonate Alkalinity is a measure of the amount of carbonate and bicarbonate anions in solution. Carbonate and bicarbonate anions contribute to alkalinity due to their basic nature, hence their ability to neutralize acid. Mathematically, the carbonate anion concentration is counted twice due to its abiliity to neutralize two protons, while bicarbonate is counted once as it can neutralize one proton.
Phenol	Phenol is an organic compound with the chemical formula C_6H_5OH. It is a white crystalline solid. The molecule consists of a phenyl (-C_6H_5), bonded to a hydroxyl (-OH) group. It is produced on a large scale (about 7 billion kg/year) as a precursor to many materials and useful compounds. It is only mildly acidic but requires careful handling due to its propensity to cause burns.

Chapter 4. FOUR - ACID-BASE CHEMISTRY

PH meter	A pH meter is an electronic instrument used for measuring the pH (acidity or alkalinity) of a liquid (though special probes are sometimes used to measure the pH of semi-solid substances). A typical pH meter consists of a special measuring probe (a glass electrode) connected to an electronic meter that measures and displays the pH reading. The probe The pH probe measures pH as the activity of hydrogen cations surrounding a thin-walled glass bulb at its tip.
Mineral	A mineral is a naturally occurring solid chemical substance that is formed through geological processes and that has a characteristic chemical composition, a highly ordered atomic structure, and specific physical properties. By comparison, a rock is an aggregate of minerals and/or mineraloids and does not have a specific chemical composition. Minerals range in composition from pure elements and simple salts to very complex silicates with thousands of known forms.
Chlorine	Chlorine (/ˈklɔːriːn/ KLOHR-een; from the Greek word 'χλωρός' (khlôros, meaning 'pale green')) is the chemical element with atomic number 17 and symbol Cl. It is a halogen, found in the periodic table in group 17. As the chloride ion, which is part of common salt and other compounds, it is abundant in nature and necessary to most forms of life, including humans. In its elemental form (Cl_2 or 'dichlorine') under standard conditions, chlorine is a powerful oxidant and is used in bleaching and disinfectants, as well as an essential reagent in the chemical industry.

PRACTICE QUIZ
Chapter 4. FOUR - ACID-BASE CHEMISTRY

1. _____ is a heterocyclic organic compound. As a bidentate ligand in coordination chemistry, it forms strong complexes with most metal ions. In terms of its coordination properties, phen is similar to 2,2'-bipyridine (bipy).

   a. Phenanthroline
   b. Safranin
   c. Tetrazolium chloride
   d. Membrane technology

2. _____ is a metallic element with a symbol Na and atomic number 11. It is a soft, silvery-white, highly reactive metal and is a member of the alkali metals within 'group 1' (formerly known as 'group IA'). It has only one stable isotope, ^{23}Na.

   Elemental _____ was first isolated by Humphry Davy in 1807 by passing an electric current through molten _____ hydroxide.

   a. 1,2-Dioxetane
   b. Sodium
   c. Chloranilic acid
   d. Counterion condensation

3. A _____ is a liquid, solid, or gas that dissolves another solid, liquid, or gaseous solute, resulting in a solution that is soluble in a certain volume of _____ at a specified temperature. Common uses for organic _____s are in dry cleaning (e.g. tetrachloroethylene), as a paint thinner (e.g. toluene, turpentine), as nail polish removers and glue _____s (acetone, methyl acetate, ethyl acetate), in spot removers (e.g. hexane, petrol ether), in detergents (citrus terpenes), in perfumes (ethanol), and in chemical synthesis. The use of inorganic _____s (other than water) is typically limited to research chemistry and some technological processes.

   a. trifluoride
   b. Betamipron
   c. Solvent
   d. Borium

4. _____ is the process of converting an atom or molecule into an ion by adding or removing charged particles such as electrons or other ions. This is often confused with dissociation. A substance may dissociate without necessarily producing ions.

----

a. ONIOM
   b. Open shell
   c. Orbital hybridisation
   d. Ionization

5. A _____ is an electronic instrument used for measuring the pH (acidity or alkalinity) of a liquid (though special probes are sometimes used to measure the pH of semi-solid substances). A typical _____ consists of a special measuring probe (a glass electrode) connected to an electronic meter that measures and displays the pH reading.

   The probe
   The pH probe measures pH as the activity of hydrogen cations surrounding a thin-walled glass bulb at its tip.

   a. PH meter
   b. Platinum black
   c. Potentiometric sensor
   d. Pourbaix diagram

ANSWER KEY
Chapter 4. FOUR - ACID-BASE CHEMISTRY

1. a
2. b
3. c
4. d
5. a

You can take the complete Chapter Practice Test

for Chapter 4. FOUR - ACID-BASE CHEMISTRY
on all key terms, persons, places, and concepts.

Online 99 Cents

http://www.epub14.6.2184.4.cram101.com/

Use www.Cram101.com for all your study needs

including Cram101's online interactive problem solving labs in chemistry, statistics, mathematics, and more.

CHAPTER OUTLINE: KEY TERMS, PEOPLE, PLACES, CONCEPTS
Chapter 5
FIVE - COORDINATION CHEMISTRY

- _____ Chemical oxygen demand
- _____ Chloride
- _____ Ethylenediaminetetraacetic acid
- _____ Hardness
- _____ Ligand
- _____ Oxygen
- _____ Conversion
- _____ Coordination number
- _____ Phenanthroline
- _____ Chemical kinetics
- _____ Instability
- _____ Dissociation
- _____ Dissociation constant
- _____ Diethylenetriamine
- _____ Electrolyte
- _____ Eriochrome Black T
- _____ Activity
- _____ Activity coefficient
- _____ Hydroxide

Chapter 5. FIVE - COORDINATION CHEMISTRY

- Solubility
- Hydrolysis
- Equilibrium constant
- Alkalinity
- Alum
- Flocculation
- Ion
- Adsorption
- Cobalt
- Silicon dioxide
- Sorption
- Seawater
- Surface water
- Agriculture
- Cadmium
- Anodic stripping voltammetry
- Copper toxicity
- Electrode
- Stripping

Chapter 5. FIVE - COORDINATION CHEMISTRY

- Voltammetry
- Cyanide
- Dimethylglyoxime
- Nitrilotriacetic acid
- Biodegradation
- Detergent
- Eutrophication
- Oxide
- Polyphosphate
- Humic acid
- Peat
- Cysteine

CHAPTER HIGHLIGHTS: KEY TERMS, PEOPLE, PLACES, CONCEPTS
Chapter 5. FIVE - COORDINATION CHEMISTRY

Chemical oxygen demand	In environmental chemistry, the chemical oxygen demand test is commonly used to indirectly measure the amount of organic compounds in water. Most applications of Chemical oxygen demand determine the amount of organic pollutants found in surface water (e.g. lakes and rivers), making Chemical oxygen demand a useful measure of water quality. It is expressed in milligrams per liter (mg/L), which indicates the mass of oxygen consumed per liter of solution.
Chloride	The chloride ion is formed when the element chlorine picks up one electron to form an anion (negatively-charged ion) Cl^-. The salts of hydrochloric acid HCl contain chloride ions and can also be called chlorides. Terminology The word chloride can also refer to a chemical compound in which one or more chlorine atoms are covalently bonded in the molecule.
Ethylenediaminetetraacetic acid	Ethylenediaminetetraacetic acid, widely abbreviated as EDTA is a polyamino carboxylic acid a colourless, water-soluble solid. Its conjugate base is named ethylenediaminetetraacetate. It widely used to dissolve scale.
Hardness	Hardness is the measure of how resistant solid matter is to various kinds of permanent shape change when a force is applied. Macroscopic hardness is generally characterized by strong intermolecular bonds, however the behavior of solid materials under force is complex, therefore there are different measurements of hardness: scratch hardness, indentation hardness, and rebound hardness. Hardness is dependent on ductility, elasticity, plasticity, strain, strength, toughness, viscoelasticity, and viscosity.
Ligand	In biochemistry and pharmacology, a ligand is a substance that forms a complex with a biomolecule to serve a biological purpose. In a narrower sense, it is a signal triggering molecule, binding to a site on a target protein.

Chapter 5. FIVE - COORDINATION CHEMISTRY

	The binding occurs by intermolecular forces, such as ionic bonds, hydrogen bonds and van der Waals forces.
Oxygen	Oxygen is the element with atomic number 8 and represented by the symbol O. At standard temperature and pressure, two atoms of the element bind to form dioxygen, a colorless, odorless, tasteless diatomic gas with the formula O_2.
	Oxygen is a member of the chalcogen group on the periodic table, and is a highly reactive nonmetallic element that readily forms compounds (notably oxides) with almost all other elements. By mass, oxygen is the third most abundant element in the universe after hydrogen and helium and the most abundant element by mass in the Earth's crust, making up almost half of the crust's mass.
Conversion	In chemistry, the phrase conversion has several meanings - specifically the property 'X' related to the yield 'Y' by multiplication with the selectivity 'S', i.e. the mathematical definition X(conversion) * S(selectivity) = Y(yield), all calculated on a molar basis; e.g. in a certain reaction, 90% of substance A is converted (consumed), but only 80% of it is converted to the desired substance B and 20% to undesired by-products, so conversion of A is 90%, selectivity for B 80% and yield of substance B 72% (= 90% * 80%) - in a general sense the action of a chemical reaction, e.g. the conversion of molecule A to molecule B; note that in this general sense, conversion rate would be synonymous with reaction rate
Coordination number	In chemistry and crystallography, the coordination number of a central atom in a molecule or crystal is the number of its nearest neighbours. This number is determined somewhat differently for molecules and for crystals.

Chapter 5. FIVE - COORDINATION CHEMISTRY

	In chemistry, the emphasis is on bonding structure in molecules or ions and the coordination number of an atom is determined by simply counting the other atoms to which it is bonded (by either single or multiple bonds).
Phenanthroline	Phenanthroline is a heterocyclic organic compound. As a bidentate ligand in coordination chemistry, it forms strong complexes with most metal ions. In terms of its coordination properties, phen is similar to 2,2'-bipyridine (bipy).
Chemical kinetics	Chemical kinetics, is the study of rates of chemical processes. Chemical kinetics includes investigations of how different experimental conditions can influence the speed of a chemical reaction and yield information about the reaction's mechanism and transition states, as well as the construction of mathematical models that can describe the characteristics of a chemical reaction. In 1864, Peter Waage and Cato Guldberg pioneered the development of chemical kinetics by formulating the law of mass action, which states that the speed of a chemical reaction is proportional to the quantity of the reacting substances.
Instability	Instability in systems is generally characterized by some of the outputs or internal states growing without bounds. Not all systems that are not stable are unstable; systems can also be marginally stable or exhibit limit cycle behavior. In control theory, a system is unstable (or as sometimes referred to as instable) if any of the roots of its characteristic equation has real part greater than zero.
Dissociation	Dissociation in chemistry and biochemistry is a general process in which ionic compounds (complexes, or salts) separate or split into smaller particles, ions, or radicals, usually in a reversible manner. When a Bronsted-Lowry acid is put in water, a covalent bond between an electronegative atom and a hydrogen atom is broken by heterolytic fission, which gives a proton and a negative ion. Dissociation is the opposite of association and recombination.
Dissociation constant	In chemistry, biochemistry, and pharmacology, a dissociation constant is a specific type of equilibrium constant that measures the propensity of a larger object to separate (dissociate) reversibly into smaller components, as when a complex falls apart into its component molecules, or when a salt splits up into its component ions. The dissociation constant is usually denoted K_d and is the inverse of the association constant. In the special case of salts, the dissociation constant can also be called an ionization constant.

Chapter 5. FIVE - COORDINATION CHEMISTRY

Diethylenetriamine	Diethylenetriamine is a colourless hygroscopic liquid, soluble in water and hydrocarbons. Diethylenetriamine is an analogue of diethylene glycol. It has similar chemical behavior as ethylene diamine and has similar uses.
Electrolyte	In chemistry, an electrolyte is any substance containing free ions that make the substance electrically conductive. The most typical electrolyte is an ionic solution, but molten electrolytes and solid electrolytes are also possible.
	Commonly, electrolytes are solutions of acids, bases or salts.
Eriochrome Black T	Eriochrome Black T is a complexometric indicator that is part of the complexometric titrations, e.g. in the water hardness determination process. It is an azo dye. It is also known as ET-00.
	In its protonated form, Eriochrome Black T is blue.
Activity	In chemical thermodynamics, activity is a measure of the 'effective concentration' of a species in a mixture. By convention, it is treated as a dimensionless quantity, although its actual value depends on customary choices of standard state for the species. The activity of pure substances in condensed phases (solid or liquids) is normally taken as unity.
Activity coefficient	An activity coefficient is a factor used in thermodynamics to account for deviations from ideal behaviour in a mixture of chemical substances. In an ideal mixture, the interactions between each pair of chemical species are the same (or more formally, the enthalpy of mixing is zero) and, as a result, properties of the mixtures can be expressed directly in terms of simple concentrations or partial pressures of the substances present e.g. Raoult's law. Deviations from ideality are accommodated by modifying the concentration by an activity coefficient.
Hydroxide	The hydroxide ion is a diatomic anion with chemical formula OH^-. It consists of an oxygen and a hydrogen atom held together by a covalent bond, and carrying a negative electrical charge. It is a natural constituent of water.

Chapter 5. FIVE - COORDINATION CHEMISTRY

Solubility	Solubility is the property of a solid, liquid, or gaseous chemical substance called solute to dissolve in a liquid solvent to form a homogeneous solution of the solute in the solvent. The solubility of a substance fundamentally depends on the used solvent as well as on temperature and pressure. The extent of the solubility of a substance in a specific solvent is measured as the saturation concentration where adding more solute does not increase the concentration of the solution.
Hydrolysis	Hydrolysis is a chemical reaction during which molecules of water (H_2O) are split into hydrogen cations (H^+, conventionally referred to as protons) and hydroxide anions (OH^-) in the process of a chemical mechanism. It is the type of reaction that is used to break down certain polymers, especially those made by condensation polymerization. Such polymer degradation is usually catalysed by either acid, e.g., concentrated sulfuric acid (H_2SO_4), or alkali, e.g., sodium hydroxide (NaOH).
Equilibrium constant	For a general chemical equilibrium $$\alpha A + \beta B ... \rightleftharpoons \sigma S + \tau T ...$$ the equilibrium constant can be defined by $$K = \frac{\{S\}^\sigma \{T\}^\tau ...}{\{A\}^\alpha \{B\}^\beta ...}$$ where {A} is the activity of the chemical species A, etc. (activity is a dimensionless quantity). It is conventional to put the activities of the products in the numerator and those of the reactants in the denominator.
Alkalinity	Alkalinity or A_T measures the ability of a solution to neutralize acids to the equivalence point of carbonate or bicarbonate. The alkalinity is equal to the stoichiometric sum of the bases in solution. In the natural environment carbonate alkalinity tends to make up most of the total alkalinity due to the common occurrence and dissolution of carbonate rocks and presence of carbon dioxide in the atmosphere.

Chapter 5. FIVE - COORDINATION CHEMISTRY

Alum	Alum is both a specific chemical compound and a class of chemical compounds. The specific compound is the hydrated potassium aluminium sulfate (Potassium alum) with the formula $KAl(SO_4)_2 \cdot 12H_2O$. The wider class of compounds known as alums have the related empirical formula, $AB(SO_4)_2 \cdot 12H_2O$. Uses Industrial Alums are useful for a range of industrial processes. They are soluble in water; have an astringent, acid, and sweetish taste; react acid to litmus; and crystallize in regular octahedra.
Flocculation	Flocculation, in the field of chemistry, is a process wherein colloids come out of suspension in the form of floc or flakes by the addition of a clarifying agent. The action differs from precipitation in that, prior to flocculation, colloids are merely suspended in a liquid and not actually dissolved in a solution. In the flocculated system, there is no formation of a cake, since all the flocs are in the suspension.
Ion	An ion is an atom or molecule in which the total number of electrons is not equal to the total number of protons, giving it a net positive or negative electrical charge. The name was given by physicist Michael Faraday for the substances that allow a current to pass ('go') between electrodes in a solution, when an electric field is applied. It is the transliteration of the Greek participle ??v, ión, 'going'.
Adsorption	Adsorption is the adhesion of atoms, ions, biomolecules or molecules of gas, liquid, or dissolved solids to a surface. This process creates a film of the adsorbate (the molecules or atoms being accumulated) on the surface of the adsorbent. It differs from absorption, in which a fluid permeates or is dissolved by a liquid or solid.
Cobalt	Cobalt is a chemical element with symbol Co and atomic number 27. It is found naturally only in chemically combined form. The free element, produced by reductive smelting, is a hard, lustrous, silver-gray metal.

Chapter 5. FIVE - COORDINATION CHEMISTRY

Cobalt-based blue pigments have been used since ancient times for jewelry and paints, and to impart a distinctive blue tint to glass, but the color was later thought by alchemists to be due to the known metal bismuth.

Silicon dioxide

The chemical compound silicon dioxide, is an oxide of silicon with the chemical formula SiO_2. It has been known for its hardness since antiquity. Silica is most commonly found in nature as sand or quartz, as well as in the cell walls of diatoms.

Sorption

Sorption refers to the action of absorption is the incorporation of a substance in one state into another of a different state (e.g., liquids being absorbed by a solid or gases being absorbed by a liquid).
- Adsorption is the physical adherence or bonding of ions and molecules onto the surface of another phase (e.g., reagents adsorbed to solid catalyst surface).

Absorption

Absorption, in chemistry, is a physical or chemical phenomenon or a process in which atoms, molecules, or ions enter some bulk phase - gas, liquid, or solid material. This is a different process from adsorption, since molecules undergoing absorption are taken up by the volume, not by the surface (as in the case for adsorption). A more general term is 'sorption', which covers absorption, adsorption, and ion exchange.

Seawater

Seawater is water from a sea or ocean. On average, seawater in the world's oceans has a salinity of about 3.5% (35 g/L, or 599 mM). This means that every kilogram (roughly one litre by volume) of seawater has approximately 35 grams (1.2 oz) of dissolved salts (predominantly Sodium Chloride ions: Na^+, Cl^-).

Surface water

Surface water is water collecting on the ground or in a stream, river, lake, wetland, or ocean; it is related to water collecting as groundwater or atmospheric water.

Chapter 5. FIVE - COORDINATION CHEMISTRY

	Surface water is naturally replenished by precipitation and naturally lost through discharge to evaporation and sub-surface seepage into the groundwater. Although there are other sources of groundwater, such as connate water and magmatic water, precipitation is the major one and groundwater originated in this way is called meteoric water.
Agriculture	Agriculture is the cultivation of animals, plants, fungi and other life forms for food, fiber, and other products used to sustain life. Agriculture was the key implement in the rise of sedentary human civilization, whereby farming of domesticated species created food surpluses that nurtured the development of civilization. The study of agriculture is known as agricultural science.
Cadmium	Cadmium is a chemical element with the symbol Cd and atomic number 48. The soft, bluish-white metal is chemically similar to the two other metals in group 12, zinc and mercury. Similar to zinc it prefers oxidation state +2 in most of its compounds and similar to mercury it shows a low melting point compared to transition metals. Cadmium and its congeners are not considered transition metals, in that they do not have partly filled d or f electron shells in the elemental or common oxidation states.
Anodic stripping voltammetry	Anodic stripping voltammetry is a voltammetric method for quantitative determination of specific ionic species. The analyte of interest is electroplated on the working electrode during a deposition step, and oxidized from the electrode during the stripping step. The current is measured during the stripping step.
Copper toxicity	Copper toxicity refers to the consequences of an excess of copper in the body. Copper toxicity can occur from eating acid food that has been cooked in un-coated copper cookware, or from exposure to excess copper in drinking water or other environmental sources. Toxicity Copper in the blood exist in two forms: bound to ceruloplasmin (85-95%) and the rest 'free' loosely bound to albumin and small molecules.

Chapter 5. FIVE - COORDINATION CHEMISTRY

Electrode	An electrode is an electrical conductor used to make contact with a nonmetallic part of a circuit (e.g. a semiconductor, an electrolyte or a vacuum). The word was coined by the scientist Michael Faraday from the Greek words elektron (meaning amber, from which the word electricity is derived) and hodos, a way.
Stripping	Stripping is a physical separation process where one or more components are removed from a liquid stream by a vapor stream. In industrial applications the liquid and vapor streams can have co-current or countercurrent flows. Stripping is usually carried out in either a packed or trayed column.
Voltammetry	Voltammetry is a category of electroanalytical methods used in analytical chemistry and various industrial processes. In voltammetry, information about an analyte is obtained by measuring the current as the potential is varied. Three electrode system Voltammetry experiments investigate the half cell reactivity of an analyte.
Cyanide	A cyanide is a chemical compound that contains the cyano group, C≡N, which consists of a carbon atom triple-bonded to a nitrogen atom. Most commonly, cyanides refers to salts of the anion CN⁻. Most cyanides are highly toxic.
Dimethylglyoxime	Dimethylglyoxime is a chemical compound described by the formula $CH_3C(NOH)C(NOH)CH_3$. This colourless solid is the dioxime derivative of the diketone diacetyl (also known as 2,3-butanedione). $DmgH_2$ is used in the analysis of palladium or nickel.
Nitrilotriacetic acid	Nitrilotriacetic acid $C_6H_9NO_6$, is a polyamino carboxylic acid and is used as a chelating agent which forms coordination compounds with metal ions (chelates) such as Ca^{2+}, Cu^{2+} or Fe^{3+}. The uses of NTA are similar to that of EDTA. However, in contrast to EDTA, NTA is easily biodegradable and is almost completely removed during wastewater treatment. In biotechnology applications it is used for protein isolation and purification.

Chapter 5. FIVE - COORDINATION CHEMISTRY

Biodegradation	Biodegradation is the chemical dissolution of materials by bacteria or other biological means. The term is often used in relation to ecology, waste management, biomedicine, and the natural environment (bioremediation) and is now commonly associated with environmentally friendly products that are capable of decomposing back into natural elements. Organic material can be degraded aerobically with oxygen, or anaerobically, without oxygen.
Detergent	A detergent is a surfactant or a mixture of surfactants having 'cleaning properties in dilute solutions.' Commonly, 'detergent' refers to alkylbenzenesulfonates, a family of compounds that are similar to soap but are less affected by hard water. In most household contexts, the term detergent by itself refers specifically to laundry detergent or dish detergent, vs hand soap or other types of cleaning agents. Detergents are commonly available as powders or concentrated solutions.
Eutrophication	Eutrophication is the addition of artificial or non-artificial substances, such as nitrates and phosphates, through fertilizers or sewage, to a fresh water system., i.e. the primary productivity of the waterbody. In other terms, it is the 'bloom' or great increase of phytoplankton in a water body. Negative environmental effects include Hypoxia, or loss of oxygen in the water with severe reductions in fish and other animal populations.
Oxide	An oxide is an anion of oxygen in the oxidation state of −2 or a chemical compound formally containing an oxygen in this state. Most of the Earth's crust consists of oxides. Oxides result when elements are oxidized by oxygen in air.
Polyphosphate	Polyphosphates are salts or esters of polymeric oxyanions formed from tetrahedral PO_4 (phosphate) structural units linked together by sharing oxygen atoms. When two corners are shared the polyphosphate may have a linear chain structure or a cyclic ring structure. In biology the polyphosphate esters AMP, ADP and ATP are involved in energy transfer.
Humic acid	Humic acid is a principal component of humic substances, which are the major organic constituents of soil (humus), peat, coal, many upland streams, dystrophic lakes, and ocean water. It is produced by biodegradation of dead organic matter. It is not a single acid; rather, it is a complex mixture of many different acids containing carboxyl and phenolate groups so that the mixture behaves functionally as a dibasic acid or, occasionally, as a tribasic acid.
Peat	Peat, is an accumulation of partially decayed vegetation matter or histosol. Peat forms in wetland bogs, moors, muskegs, pocosins, mires, and peat swamp forests. Peat is harvested as an important source of fuel in certain parts of the world.

Chapter 5. FIVE - COORDINATION CHEMISTRY

Cysteine	Cysteine is an α-amino acid with the chemical formula $HO_2CCH(NH_2)CH_2SH$. It is a non-essential amino acid, which means that it is biosynthesized in humans. Its codons are UGU and UGC. The side chain on cysteine is thiol, which is nonpolar and thus cysteine is usually classified as a hydrophobic amino acid. The thiol side chain often participates in enzymatic reactions, serving as a nucleophile.

PRACTICE QUIZ
Chapter 5. FIVE - COORDINATION CHEMISTRY

1. _____ is both a specific chemical compound and a class of chemical compounds. The specific compound is the hydrated potassium aluminium sulfate (Potassium _____) with the formula KAl(SO$_4$)$_2$·12H$_2$O. The wider class of compounds known as _____s have the related empirical formula, AB(SO$_4$)$_2$·12H$_2$O.

   Uses

   Industrial

   _____s are useful for a range of industrial processes. They are soluble in water; have an astringent, acid, and sweetish taste; react acid to litmus; and crystallize in regular octahedra.

   a. Isomer
   b. Alum
   c. Air conditioning
   d. Oxyanion

2. _____ is the chemical dissolution of materials by bacteria or other biological means. The term is often used in relation to ecology, waste management, biomedicine, and the natural environment (bioremediation) and is now commonly associated with environmentally friendly products that are capable of decomposing back into natural elements. Organic material can be degraded aerobically with oxygen, or anaerobically, without oxygen.

   a. 1,2-Dioxetane
   b. Biodegradation
   c. Polyamino carboxylic acid
   d. Tetramethylethylenediamine

3. _____, is the study of rates of chemical processes. _____ includes investigations of how different experimental conditions can influence the speed of a chemical reaction and yield information about the reaction's mechanism and transition states, as well as the construction of mathematical models that can describe the characteristics of a chemical reaction. In 1864, Peter Waage and Cato Guldberg pioneered the development of _____ by formulating the law of mass action, which states that the speed of a chemical reaction is proportional to the quantity of the reacting substances.

   a. Kinetic capillary electrophoresis
   b. Reactions on surfaces
   c. Chemical kinetics
   d. Catalysis

----

4. In chemical thermodynamics, _____ is a measure of the 'effective concentration' of a species in a mixture. By convention, it is treated as a dimensionless quantity, although its actual value depends on customary choices of standard state for the species. The _____ of pure substances in condensed phases (solid or liquids) is normally taken as unity.

   a. Enthalpy of sublimation
   b. Enthalpy of fusion
   c. Isomer
   d. Activity

5. For a general chemical equilibrium

$$\alpha A + \beta B ... \rightleftharpoons \sigma S + \tau T ...$$

   the _____ can be defined by

$$K = \frac{\{S\}^\sigma \{T\}^\tau ...}{\{A\}^\alpha \{B\}^\beta ...}$$

   where {A} is the activity of the chemical species A, etc. (activity is a dimensionless quantity). It is conventional to put the activities of the products in the numerator and those of the reactants in the denominator.

   a. Equilibrium unfolding
   b. ICE table
   c. Equilibrium constant
   d. Oxyanion

ANSWER KEY
Chapter 5. FIVE - COORDINATION CHEMISTRY

1. b
2. b
3. c
4. d
5. c

You can take the complete Chapter Practice Test

for Chapter 5. FIVE - COORDINATION CHEMISTRY
on all key terms, persons, places, and concepts.

Online 99 Cents

http://www.epub14.6.2184.5.cram101.com/

Use www.Cram101.com for all your study needs

including Cram101's online interactive problem solving labs in chemistry, statistics, mathematics, and more.

CHAPTER OUTLINE: KEY TERMS, PEOPLE, PLACES, CONCEPTS
Chapter 6
SIX - PRECIPITATION AND DISSOLUTION

- Solubility
- Hydroxide
- Calcite
- Calcium
- Calcium carbonate
- Nucleation
- Precipitation
- Dissolution
- Crystal growth
- Particle size
- Groundwater
- Product
- Activity
- Activity coefficient
- Equilibrium constant
- Calcium fluoride
- Chloride
- Silver chloride
- Silver chromate

Chapter 6. SIX - PRECIPITATION AND DISSOLUTION

- Fluoride
- Calcium sulfate
- Oxide
- Amorphous carbon
- Cadmium
- Cadmium hydroxide
- Calcium hydroxide
- Magnesium
- Magnesium hydroxide
- Concentration
- Acid salt
- Cyanide
- Sodium chloride
- Weak acid
- Weak base
- Seawater
- Alum
- Ferrous
- Ligand

Chapter 6. SIX - PRECIPITATION AND DISSOLUTION

- Wastewater
- Alkalinity
- Hardness
- Closed system
- Saturation
- Chemical kinetics
- Reaction rate
- Cathodic protection
- Coating
- Ethylenediaminetetraacetic acid
- Detergent
- Polyphosphate
- Sodium
- Hydrolysis
- Pyrophosphoric acid
- Hydroxylapatite
- Amorphous solid
- Induction period
- Period

Chapter 6. SIX - PRECIPITATION AND DISSOLUTION

- Ammonium
- Ammonium phosphate
- Anaerobic digestion
- Digestion
- X-ray crystallography
- Crystallography

CHAPTER HIGHLIGHTS: KEY TERMS, PEOPLE, PLACES, CONCEPTS
Chapter 6. SIX - PRECIPITATION AND DISSOLUTION

Solubility	Solubility is the property of a solid, liquid, or gaseous chemical substance called solute to dissolve in a liquid solvent to form a homogeneous solution of the solute in the solvent. The solubility of a substance fundamentally depends on the used solvent as well as on temperature and pressure. The extent of the solubility of a substance in a specific solvent is measured as the saturation concentration where adding more solute does not increase the concentration of the solution.
Hydroxide	The hydroxide ion is a diatomic anion with chemical formula OH^-. It consists of an oxygen and a hydrogen atom held together by a covalent bond, and carrying a negative electrical charge. It is a natural constituent of water.
Calcite	Calcite is a carbonate mineral and the most stable polymorph of calcium carbonate ($CaCO_3$). The other polymorphs are the minerals aragonite and vaterite. Aragonite will change to calcite at 470 °C, and vaterite is even less stable.
Calcium	Calcium is the chemical element with the symbol Ca and atomic number 20. It has an atomic mass of 40.078 amu. Calcium is a soft gray alkaline earth metal, and is the fifth most abundant element by mass in the Earth's crust. Calcium is also the fifth most abundant dissolved ion in seawater by both molarity and mass, after sodium, chloride, magnesium, and sulfate.
Calcium carbonate	Calcium carbonate is a chemical compound with the formula $CaCO_3$. It is a common substance found in rocks in all parts of the world, and is the main component of shells of marine organisms, snails, pearls, and eggshells. Calcium carbonate is the active ingredient in agricultural lime, and is usually the principal cause of hard water.
Nucleation	Nucleation is the extremely localized budding of a distinct thermodynamic phase. Some examples of phases that may form via nucleation in liquids are gaseous bubbles, crystals or glassy regions. Creation of liquid droplets in saturated vapor is also characterized by nucleation.
Precipitation	Precipitation is the formation of a solid in a solution or inside another solid during a chemical reaction or by diffusion in a solid. When the reaction occurs in a liquid, the solid formed is called the precipitate, or when compacted by a centrifuge, a pellet. The liquid remaining above the solid is in either case called the supernate or supernatant.
Dissolution	Dissolution is the process by which a solid or liquid forms a solution in a solvent. In solids this can be explained as the breakdown of the crystal lattice into individual ions, atoms or molecules and their transport into the solvent. Dissolution testing is widely used in the pharmaceutical industry for optimization of formulation and quality control.

Chapter 6. SIX - PRECIPITATION AND DISSOLUTION

Crystal growth	A crystal is a solid material whose constituent atoms, molecules, or ions are arranged in an orderly repeating pattern extending in all three spatial dimensions. Crystal growth is a major stage of a crystallization process, and consists in the addition of new atoms, ions, or polymer strings into the characteristic arrangement of a crystalline Bravais lattice. The growth typically follows an initial stage of either homogeneous or heterogeneous (surface catalyzed) nucleation, unless a 'seed' crystal, purposely added to start the growth, was already present.
Particle size	Particle size is a notion introduced for comparings dimensions of solid particles (flecks), liquid particles (droplets), or gaseous particles (bubbles). The notion of particle size applies to - Colloidal particles; - Particles in ecology; - Particles present in particulate matter; - Particles that form a granular material. The particle size of a spherical object can be unambiguously and quantitatively defined by its diameter. However, a typical material object is likely to be irregular in shape and non-spherical.
Groundwater	Groundwater is water located beneath the ground surface in soil pore spaces and in the fractures of rock formations. A unit of rock or an unconsolidated deposit is called an aquifer when it can yield a usable quantity of water. The depth at which soil pore spaces or fractures and voids in rock become completely saturated with water is called the water table.
Product	Product(s) are formed during chemical reactions as reagents are consumed. Products have lower energy than the reagents and are produced during the reaction according to the second law of thermodynamics. The released energy comes from changes in chemical bonds between atoms in reagent molecules and may be given off in the form of heat or light.

Chapter 6. SIX - PRECIPITATION AND DISSOLUTION

Activity	In chemical thermodynamics, activity is a measure of the 'effective concentration' of a species in a mixture. By convention, it is treated as a dimensionless quantity, although its actual value depends on customary choices of standard state for the species. The activity of pure substances in condensed phases (solid or liquids) is normally taken as unity.
Activity coefficient	An activity coefficient is a factor used in thermodynamics to account for deviations from ideal behaviour in a mixture of chemical substances. In an ideal mixture, the interactions between each pair of chemical species are the same (or more formally, the enthalpy of mixing is zero) and, as a result, properties of the mixtures can be expressed directly in terms of simple concentrations or partial pressures of the substances present e.g. Raoult's law. Deviations from ideality are accommodated by modifying the concentration by an activity coefficient.
Equilibrium constant	For a general chemical equilibrium $$\alpha A + \beta B ... \rightleftharpoons \sigma S + \tau T ...$$ the equilibrium constant can be defined by $$K = \frac{\{S\}^{\sigma}\{T\}^{\tau}...}{\{A\}^{\alpha}\{B\}^{\beta}...}$$ where {A} is the activity of the chemical species A, etc. (activity is a dimensionless quantity). It is conventional to put the activities of the products in the numerator and those of the reactants in the denominator.
Calcium fluoride	Calcium fluoride is the inorganic compound with the formula CaF_2. This ionic compound of calcium and fluorine occurs naturally as the mineral fluorite (also called fluorspar). It is the source of most of the world's fluorine.
Chloride	The chloride ion is formed when the element chlorine picks up one electron to form an anion (negatively-charged ion) Cl^-. The salts of hydrochloric acid HCl contain chloride ions and can also be called chlorides. Terminology

----

Chapter 6. SIX - PRECIPITATION AND DISSOLUTION

	The word chloride can also refer to a chemical compound in which one or more chlorine atoms are covalently bonded in the molecule.
Silver chloride	Silver chloride is a chemical compound with the chemical formula AgCl. This white crystalline solid is well known for its low solubility in water (this behavior being reminiscent of the chlorides of Tl^+ and Pb^{2+}). Upon illumination or heating, silver chloride converts to silver (and chlorine), which is signalled by greyish or purplish coloration to some samples.
Silver chromate	Silver chromate is a brown-red monoclinic crystal and is a chemical precursor to modern photography. It can be formed by combining silver nitrate ($AgNO_3$) and potassium chromate (K_2CrO_4). This reaction has been important in neuroscience, as it is used in the 'Golgi method' of staining neurons for microscopy: the silver chromate produced precipitates inside neurons and makes their morphology visible.
Fluoride	Fluoride is the anion F^-, the reduced form of fluorine when as an ion and when bonded to another element. Both organofluorine compounds and inorganic fluorine compounds containing are called fluorides. Fluoride, like other halides, is a monovalent ion (−1 charge).
Calcium sulfate	Calcium sulfate is a common laboratory and industrial chemical. In the form of γ-anhydrite (the nearly anhydrous form), it is used as a desiccant. It is also used as a coagulant in products like tofu.
Oxide	An oxide is an anion of oxygen in the oxidation state of −2 or a chemical compound formally containing an oxygen in this state. Most of the Earth's crust consists of oxides. Oxides result when elements are oxidized by oxygen in air.
Amorphous carbon	Amorphous carbon, reactive carbon, is an allotrope of carbon that does not have any crystalline structure. As with all glassy materials, some short-range order can be observed. Amorphous carbon is often abbreviated to aC for general amorphous carbon, aC:H for hydrogenated amorphous carbon, or to ta-C for tetrahedral amorphous carbon.
Cadmium	Cadmium is a chemical element with the symbol Cd and atomic number 48. The soft, bluish-white metal is chemically similar to the two other metals in group 12, zinc and mercury. Similar to zinc it prefers oxidation state +2 in most of its compounds and similar to mercury it shows a low melting point compared to transition metals. Cadmium and its congeners are not considered transition metals, in that they do not have partly filled d or f electron shells in the elemental or common oxidation states.

Chapter 6. SIX - PRECIPITATION AND DISSOLUTION

Cadmium hydroxide	Cadmium hydroxide is an inorganic compound with the formula $Cd(OH)_2$. It is a white crystalline ionic compound that is a key component of NiCd batteries. Preparation and reactions Cadmium hydroxide is produced by treating cadmium nitrate with sodium hydroxide: $$Cd(NO_3)_2 + 2\ NaOH \rightarrow Cd(OH)_2 + 2\ NaNO_3$$ Attempted preparation from other cadmium salts is more complicated.
Calcium hydroxide	Calcium hydroxide, traditionally called slaked lime, is an inorganic compound with the chemical formula $Ca(OH)_2$. It is a colourless crystal or white powder and is obtained when calcium oxide (called lime or quicklime) is mixed, or 'slaked' with water. It has many names including hydrated lime, builders lime, slack lime, cal, or pickling lime.
Magnesium	Magnesium is a chemical element with the symbol Mg, atomic number 12 and common oxidation number +2. It is an alkaline earth metal and the eighth most abundant element in the Earth's crust, where it constitutes about 2% by mass, and ninth in the known Universe as a whole. This preponderance of magnesium is related to the fact that it is easily built up in supernova stars from a sequential addition of three helium nuclei to carbon (which in turn is made from three helium nuclei). Magnesium ion's high solubility in water helps ensure that it is the third most abundant element dissolved in seawater.
Magnesium hydroxide	Magnesium hydroxide is an inorganic compound with the chemical formula $Mg(OH)_2$. As a suspension in water, it is often called milk of magnesia because of its milk-like appearance. The solid mineral form of magnesium hydroxide is known as brucite.
Concentration	In chemistry, concentration is defined as the abundance of a constituent divided by the total volume of a mixture. Furthermore, in chemistry, four types of mathematical description can be distinguished: mass concentration, molar concentration, number concentration, and volume concentration. The term concentration can be applied to any kind of chemical mixture, but most frequently it refers to solutes in solutions.

Chapter 6. SIX - PRECIPITATION AND DISSOLUTION

Acid salt	Acid salt is a somewhat obscure term for a class of salts formed by the partial neutralization of diprotic or polyprotic acids. Because the parent acid is only partially neutralized, one or more replaceable hydrogen ions remain. Typical acid salts have one or more alkali (alkaline) metal ions as well as one or more protons.
Cyanide	A cyanide is a chemical compound that contains the cyano group, C≡N, which consists of a carbon atom triple-bonded to a nitrogen atom. Most commonly, cyanides refers to salts of the anion CN$^-$. Most cyanides are highly toxic.
Sodium chloride	Sodium chloride, common salt, table salt, or halite, is an ionic compound with the formula NaCl. Sodium chloride is the salt most responsible for the salinity of the ocean and of the extracellular fluid of many multicellular organisms. As the major ingredient in edible salt, it is commonly used as a condiment and food preservative.
Weak acid	A weak acid is an acid that dissociates incompletely. It does not release all of its hydrogens in a solution, donating only a partial amount of its protons to the solution. These acids have higher pKa than strong acids, which release all of their hydrogen atoms when dissolved in water.
Weak base	In chemistry, a weak base is a chemical base that does not ionize fully in an aqueous solution. As Bronsted-Lowry bases are proton acceptors, a weak base may also be defined as a chemical base in which protonation is incomplete. This results in a relatively low pH level compared to strong bases.
Seawater	Seawater is water from a sea or ocean. On average, seawater in the world's oceans has a salinity of about 3.5% (35 g/L, or 599 mM). This means that every kilogram (roughly one litre by volume) of seawater has approximately 35 grams (1.2 oz) of dissolved salts (predominantly Sodium Chloride ions: Na$^+$, Cl$^-$).
Alum	Alum is both a specific chemical compound and a class of chemical compounds. The specific compound is the hydrated potassium aluminium sulfate (Potassium alum) with the formula KAl(SO$_4$)$_2$·12H$_2$O. The wider class of compounds known as alums have the related empirical formula, AB(SO$_4$)$_2$·12H$_2$O. Uses Industrial

----

Chapter 6. SIX - PRECIPITATION AND DISSOLUTION

	Alums are useful for a range of industrial processes. They are soluble in water; have an astringent, acid, and sweetish taste; react acid to litmus; and crystallize in regular octahedra.
Ferrous	Ferrous chemical science, indicates a bivalent iron compound (+2 oxidation state), as opposed to ferric, which indicates a trivalent iron compound (+3 oxidation state).
	Outside of chemical science, ferrous is an adjective used to indicate the presence of iron. Ferrous metals include steel and pig iron (with a carbon content of a few percent) and alloys of iron with other metals (such as stainless steel).
Ligand	In biochemistry and pharmacology, a ligand is a substance that forms a complex with a biomolecule to serve a biological purpose. In a narrower sense, it is a signal triggering molecule, binding to a site on a target protein.
	The binding occurs by intermolecular forces, such as ionic bonds, hydrogen bonds and van der Waals forces.
Wastewater	Wastewater is any water that has been adversely affected in quality by anthropogenic influence. It comprises liquid waste discharged by domestic residences, commercial properties, industry, and/or agriculture and can encompass a wide range of potential contaminants and concentrations. In the most common usage, it refers to the municipal wastewater that contains a broad spectrum of contaminants resulting from the mixing of wastewaters from different sources.
Alkalinity	Alkalinity or A_T measures the ability of a solution to neutralize acids to the equivalence point of carbonate or bicarbonate. The alkalinity is equal to the stoichiometric sum of the bases in solution. In the natural environment carbonate alkalinity tends to make up most of the total alkalinity due to the common occurrence and dissolution of carbonate rocks and presence of carbon dioxide in the atmosphere.

Chapter 6. SIX - PRECIPITATION AND DISSOLUTION

Hardness	Hardness is the measure of how resistant solid matter is to various kinds of permanent shape change when a force is applied. Macroscopic hardness is generally characterized by strong intermolecular bonds, however the behavior of solid materials under force is complex, therefore there are different measurements of hardness: scratch hardness, indentation hardness, and rebound hardness. Hardness is dependent on ductility, elasticity, plasticity, strain, strength, toughness, viscoelasticity, and viscosity.
Closed system	The term closed system has different meanings in different contexts. In computing In computing a closed system refers to software which the specifications and detail of implementation (typically source code) are kept secret, as opposed to open source systems. In physics In thermodynamics, a closed system can exchange heat and work (for example, energy), but not matter, with its surroundings.
Saturation	In chemistry, saturation has six different meanings, all based on reaching a maximum capacity 1. In physical chemistry, saturation is the point at which a solution of a substance can dissolve no more of that substance and additional amounts of it will appear as a precipitate. This point of maximum concentration, the saturation point, depends on the temperature of the liquid as well as the chemical nature of the substances involved. This can be used in the process of recrystallisation to purify a chemical: it is dissolved to the point of saturation in hot solvent, then as the solvent cools and the solubility decreases, excess solute precipitates.

Chapter 6. SIX - PRECIPITATION AND DISSOLUTION

Chemical kinetics	Chemical kinetics, is the study of rates of chemical processes. Chemical kinetics includes investigations of how different experimental conditions can influence the speed of a chemical reaction and yield information about the reaction's mechanism and transition states, as well as the construction of mathematical models that can describe the characteristics of a chemical reaction. In 1864, Peter Waage and Cato Guldberg pioneered the development of chemical kinetics by formulating the law of mass action, which states that the speed of a chemical reaction is proportional to the quantity of the reacting substances.
Reaction rate	The reaction rate is intuitively defined as how fast or slow a reaction takes place. For example, the oxidation of iron under the atmosphere is a slow reaction which can take many years, but the combustion of butane in a fire is a reaction that takes place in fractions of a second. Chemical kinetics is the part of physical chemistry that studies reaction rates.
Cathodic protection	Cathodic protection is a technique used to control the corrosion of a metal surface by making it the cathode of an electrochemical cell. The simplest method to apply cathodic\ protection is by connecting the metal to be protected with another more easily corroded 'sacrificial metal' to act as the anode of the electrochemical cell. Cathodic protection systems are used to protect a wide range of metallic structures in various environments.
Coating	Coating is a covering that is applied to the surface of an object, usually referred to as the substrate. In many cases coatings are applied to improve surface properties of the substrate, such as appearance, adhesion, wetability, corrosion resistance, wear resistance, and scratch resistance. In other cases, in particular in printing processes and semiconductor device fabrication (where the substrate is a wafer), the coating forms an essential part of the finished product.
Ethylenediaminetetraacetic acid	Ethylenediaminetetraacetic acid, widely abbreviated as EDTA is a polyamino carboxylic acid a colourless, water-soluble solid. Its conjugate base is named ethylenediaminetetraacetate. It widely used to dissolve scale.
Detergent	A detergent is a surfactant or a mixture of surfactants having 'cleaning properties in dilute solutions.' Commonly, 'detergent' refers to alkylbenzenesulfonates, a family of compounds that are similar to soap but are less affected by hard water. In most household contexts, the term detergent by itself refers specifically to laundry detergent or dish detergent, vs hand soap or other types of cleaning agents. Detergents are commonly available as powders or concentrated solutions.

Chapter 6. SIX - PRECIPITATION AND DISSOLUTION

Polyphosphate	Polyphosphates are salts or esters of polymeric oxyanions formed from tetrahedral PO_4 (phosphate) structural units linked together by sharing oxygen atoms. When two corners are shared the polyphosphate may have a linear chain structure or a cyclic ring structure. In biology the polyphosphate esters AMP, ADP and ATP are involved in energy transfer.
Sodium	Sodium is a metallic element with a symbol Na and atomic number 11. It is a soft, silvery-white, highly reactive metal and is a member of the alkali metals within 'group 1' (formerly known as 'group IA'). It has only one stable isotope, ^{23}Na. Elemental sodium was first isolated by Humphry Davy in 1807 by passing an electric current through molten sodium hydroxide.
Hydrolysis	Hydrolysis is a chemical reaction during which molecules of water (H_2O) are split into hydrogen cations (H^+, conventionally referred to as protons) and hydroxide anions (OH^-) in the process of a chemical mechanism. It is the type of reaction that is used to break down certain polymers, especially those made by condensation polymerization. Such polymer degradation is usually catalysed by either acid, e.g., concentrated sulfuric acid (H_2SO_4), or alkali, e.g., sodium hydroxide (NaOH).
Pyrophosphoric acid	Pyrophosphoric acid, also known under the name diphosphoric acid, is colorless, odorless, hygroscopic and is soluble in water, diethyl ether, and ethyl alcohol. It is produced from phosphoric acid by dehydration. Pyrophosphoric acid slowly hydrolyzes in the presence of water into phosphoric acid.
Hydroxylapatite	Hydroxylapatite, is a naturally occurring mineral form of calcium apatite with the formula $Ca_5(PO_4)_3(OH)$, but is usually written $Ca_{10}(PO_4)_6(OH)_2$ to denote that the crystal unit cell comprises two entities. Hydroxylapatite is the hydroxyl endmember of the complex apatite group. The OH^- ion can be replaced by fluoride, chloride or carbonate, producing fluorapatite or chlorapatite.
Amorphous solid	In condensed matter physics, an amorphous or non-crystalline solid is a solid that lacks the long-range order characteristic of a crystal.

Chapter 6. SIX - PRECIPITATION AND DISSOLUTION

	In part of the older literature, the term has been used synonymously with glass. Nowadays, 'amorphous solid' is considered to be the overarching concept, and 'glass' the more special case: A glass is an amorphous solid that transforms into a liquid upon heating through the glass transition.
Induction period	An induction period in chemical kinetics is an initial slow stage of a chemical reaction; after the induction period, the reaction accelerates. Ignoring induction periods can lead to runaway reactions.
	In some catalytic reactions, a pre-catalyst needs to undergo a transformation to form the active catalyst, before the catalyst can take effect.
Period	In the periodic table of the elements, elements are arranged in a series of rows (or periods) so that those with similar properties appear in vertical columns. Elements of the same period have the same number of electron shells; with each group across a period, the elements have one more proton and electron and become less metallic. This arrangement reflects the periodic recurrence of similar properties as the atomic number increases.
Ammonium	The ammonium cation is a positively charged polyatomic cation with the chemical formula NH_4^+. It is formed by the protonation of ammonia (NH_3). Ammonium is also a general name for positively charged or protonated substituted amines and quaternary ammonium cations (N^+R_4), where one or more hydrogen atoms are replaced by organic radical groups (indicated by R).
Ammonium phosphate	Ammonium phosphate is the salt of ammonia and phosphoric acid. It has the formula $(NH_4)_3PO_4$ and consists of ammonium cations and phosphate anion. It is obtained as a crystalline powder upon mixing concentrated solutions of ammonia and phosphoric acid, or on the addition of excess of ammonia to the acid phosphate $(NH_4)_2(HPO_4)$.
Anaerobic digestion	Anaerobic digestion is a series of processes in which microorganisms break down biodegradable material in the absence of oxygen, used for industrial or domestic purposes to manage waste and/or to release energy.

Chapter 6. SIX - PRECIPITATION AND DISSOLUTION

	It is widely used as part of the process to treat wastewater. As part of an integrated waste management system, anaerobic digestion reduces the emission of landfill gas into the atmosphere.
Digestion	In alchemy, Digestion is a process in which gentle heat is applied to a substance over a period of several weeks.
	This was traditionally performed by sealing a sample of the substance in a flask, and keeping the flask in fresh horse dung or sometimes in direct sunlight. Today, practitioners of alchemy use thermostat-controlled incubators.
X-ray crystallography	X-ray crystallography is a method of determining the arrangement of atoms within a crystal, in which a beam of X-rays strikes a crystal and diffracts into many specific directions. From the angles and intensities of these diffracted beams, a crystallographer can produce a three-dimensional picture of the density of electrons within the crystal. From this electron density, the mean positions of the atoms in the crystal can be determined, as well as their chemical bonds, their disorder and various other information.
Crystallography	Crystallography is the science of the arrangement of atoms in solids. The word 'crystallography' derives from the Greek words crystallon = cold drop / frozen drop, with its meaning extending to all solids with some degree of transparency, and grapho = write.

PRACTICE QUIZ
Chapter 6. SIX - PRECIPITATION AND DISSOLUTION

1. _____, reactive carbon, is an allotrope of carbon that does not have any crystalline structure. As with all glassy materials, some short-range order can be observed. _____ is often abbreviated to aC for general _____, aC:H for hydrogenated _____, or to ta-C for tetrahedral _____.

   a. Atomic carbon
   b. Isomer
   c. Amorphous carbon
   d. Potassium hexacyanochromate

2. _____ is the property of a solid, liquid, or gaseous chemical substance called solute to dissolve in a liquid solvent to form a homogeneous solution of the solute in the solvent. The _____ of a substance fundamentally depends on the used solvent as well as on temperature and pressure. The extent of the _____ of a substance in a specific solvent is measured as the saturation concentration where adding more solute does not increase the concentration of the solution.

   a. 1,2-Dioxetane
   b. 1,3,5-Trioxane
   c. Chloranilic acid
   d. Solubility

3. _____ is water located beneath the ground surface in soil pore spaces and in the fractures of rock formations. A unit of rock or an unconsolidated deposit is called an aquifer when it can yield a usable quantity of water. The depth at which soil pore spaces or fractures and voids in rock become completely saturated with water is called the water table.

   a. Hydraulic head
   b. 1,2-Dioxetane
   c. 1,3,5-Trioxane
   d. Groundwater

4. The _____ ion is a diatomic anion with chemical formula OH^-. It consists of an oxygen and a hydrogen atom held together by a covalent bond, and carrying a negative electrical charge. It is a natural constituent of water.

   a. Nucleosol
   b. 1,2-Dioxetane
   c. Hydroxide
   d. Chloranilic acid

5. _____ is a carbonate mineral and the most stable polymorph of calcium carbonate ($CaCO_3$). The other polymorphs are the minerals aragonite and vaterite. Aragonite will change to _____ at 470 °C, and vaterite is even less stable.

   a. Kota Stone
   b. Calcite
   c. 1,2-Dioxetane
   d. 1,3,5-Trioxane

ANSWER KEY
Chapter 6. SIX - PRECIPITATION AND DISSOLUTION

1. c
2. d
3. d
4. c
5. b

You can take the complete Chapter Practice Test

for Chapter 6. SIX - PRECIPITATION AND DISSOLUTION
on all key terms, persons, places, and concepts.

Online 99 Cents

http://www.epub14.6.2184.6.cram101.com/

Use www.Cram101.com for all your study needs

including Cram101's online interactive problem solving labs in chemistry, statistics, mathematics, and more.

CHAPTER OUTLINE: KEY TERMS, PEOPLE, PLACES, CONCEPTS
Chapter 7
SEVEN - OXIDATION - REDUCTION REACTIONS

- _____ Redox
- _____ Half-reaction
- _____ Stoichiometry
- _____ Nernst equation
- _____ Chemical oxygen demand
- _____ Equivalent weight
- _____ Ozone
- _____ Reducing agent
- _____ Oxygen
- _____ Periodic table
- _____ Permanganate
- _____ Calcium
- _____ Calcium hypochlorite
- _____ Chlorine
- _____ Sodium
- _____ Sodium hypochlorite
- _____ Hypochlorite
- _____ Ferrous
- _____ Amorphous carbon

Chapter 7. SEVEN - OXIDATION - REDUCTION REACTIONS

- Ammonium
- Ammonium sulfate
- Reduction potential
- Reaction quotient
- Dissolution
- Sodium thiosulfate
- Thiosulfate
- Electrochemical cell
- Ethylenediaminetetraacetic acid
- Galvanic cell
- Hydrogen
- Electrode
- Equilibrium constant
- Standard electrode potential
- Electrode potential
- Daniell cell
- Activity
- Corrosion
- Peat

Chapter 7. SEVEN - OXIDATION - REDUCTION REACTIONS

- Solubility
- Bromine
- Boltzmann constant
- Sunlight
- Iodine
- Anode
- Cathodic protection
- Embrittlement
- Cathode
- Galvanic series
- Seawater
- Atomic number
- Atomic weight
- Concentration
- Concentration cell
- Intensity
- Calcite
- Calcium carbonate
- Passivation

Chapter 7. SEVEN - OXIDATION - REDUCTION REACTIONS

- Coating
- Material
- Oxide
- Precipitation
- Saturation
- Deoxygenation
- Pyrite
- Chemical kinetics
- Hypochlorous acid
- Ammonia
- Chloramine
- Nitrite
- Polysulfide
- Hydrazine
- Hydroxylamine
- Nitrogen
- Nitrogen trichloride
- Methylamine
- Phenol

Chapter 7. SEVEN - OXIDATION - REDUCTION REACTIONS

- Chloroform
- Trihalomethane
- Acetone
- Oxalic acid
- Biosynthesis
- Catalysis
- Amination
- Deamination
- Nitrate
- Nitrogen cycle
- Fixation
- Rhizobium
- Acceptor
- Electron acceptor
- Formaldehyde
- Activated sludge
- Fermentation
- Methane
- Sludge

Chapter 7. SEVEN - OXIDATION - REDUCTION REACTIONS

- Carbon
- Adsorption
- Anaerobic digestion
- Digestion
- Liquid
- Reference electrode
- Sodium chloride
- Salt bridge
- Saturated calomel electrode
- Silver chloride electrode
- Glass electrode
- PH meter
- Divalent
- Polarization
- Dropping mercury electrode
- Absorption
- Mercury
- Spectrophotometry
- Amperometric titration

Chapter 7. SEVEN - OXIDATION - REDUCTION REACTIONS

_____ Titration

_____ Ionization

_____ Product

CHAPTER HIGHLIGHTS: KEY TERMS, PEOPLE, PLACES, CONCEPTS
Chapter 7. SEVEN - OXIDATION - REDUCTION REACTIONS

Redox	Redox reactions describe all chemical reactions in which atoms have their oxidation number (oxidation state) changed. This can be either a simple redox process, such as the oxidation of carbon to yield carbon dioxide (CO_2) or the reduction of carbon by hydrogen to yield methane (CH_4), or a complex process such as the oxidation of sugar ($C_6H_{12}O_6$) in the human body through a series of complex electron transfer processes. The term comes from the two concepts of reduction and oxidation.
Half-reaction	A half reaction is either the oxidation or reduction reaction component of a redox reaction. A half reaction is obtained by considering the change in oxidation states of individual substances involved in the redox reaction. Example Consider the reaction below: $$Cl_2 + 2Fe^{2+} \rightarrow 2Cl^- + 2Fe^{3+}$$ The two elements involved, iron and chlorine, each change oxidation state; iron from 2+ to 3+, chlorine from 0 to 1−. There are then effectively two half-reactions occurring.
Stoichiometry	Stoichiometry is a branch of chemistry that deals with the relative quantities of reactants and products in chemical reactions. In a balanced chemical reaction, the relations among quantities of reactants and products typically form a ratio of whole numbers. For example, in a reaction that forms ammonia (NH_3), exactly one molecule of nitrogen (N_2) reacts with three molecules of hydrogen (H_2) to produce two molecules of NH_3: $$N_2 + 3H_2 \rightarrow 2NH_3$$ Stoichiometry can be used to calculate quantities such as the amount of products (in mass, moles, volume, etc).

Chapter 7. SEVEN - OXIDATION - REDUCTION REACTIONS

Nernst equation	In electrochemistry, the Nernst equation is an equation that can be used (in conjunction with other information) to determine the equilibrium reduction potential of a half-cell in an electrochemical cell. It can also be used to determine the total voltage (electromotive force) for a full electrochemical cell. It is named after the German physical chemist who first formulated it, Walther Nernst.
Chemical oxygen demand	In environmental chemistry, the chemical oxygen demand test is commonly used to indirectly measure the amount of organic compounds in water. Most applications of Chemical oxygen demand determine the amount of organic pollutants found in surface water (e.g. lakes and rivers), making Chemical oxygen demand a useful measure of water quality. It is expressed in milligrams per liter (mg/L), which indicates the mass of oxygen consumed per liter of solution.
Equivalent weight	Equivalent weight is a term which has been used in several contexts in chemistry. In its most general usage, it is the mass of one equivalent, that is the mass of a given substance which will: • supply or react with one mole of hydrogen ions (H^+) in an acid-base reaction; or • supply or react with one mole of electrons in a redox reaction. Equivalent weight has the dimensions and units of mass, unlike atomic weight, which is dimensionless. Equivalent weights were originally determined by experiment, but (insofar as they are still used) are now derived from molar masses.
Ozone	Ozone, is a triatomic molecule, consisting of three oxygen atoms. It is an allotrope of oxygen that is much less stable than the diatomic allotrope (O_2). Ozone in the lower atmosphere is an air pollutant with harmful effects on the respiratory systems of animals and will burn sensitive plants; however, the ozone layer in the upper atmosphere is beneficial, preventing potentially damaging ultraviolet light from reaching the Earth's surface.
Reducing agent	A reducing agent is the element or compound in a reduction-oxidation (redox) reaction that donates an electron to another species; however, since the reducer loses an electron we say it is 'oxidized'. This means that there must be an 'oxidizer'; because if any chemical is an electron donor (reducer), another must be an electron recipient (oxidizer). Thus reducers are 'oxidized' and oxidizers are 'reduced'.

Chapter 7. SEVEN - OXIDATION - REDUCTION REACTIONS

Oxygen	Oxygen is the element with atomic number 8 and represented by the symbol O. At standard temperature and pressure, two atoms of the element bind to form dioxygen, a colorless, odorless, tasteless diatomic gas with the formula O_2.
	Oxygen is a member of the chalcogen group on the periodic table, and is a highly reactive nonmetallic element that readily forms compounds (notably oxides) with almost all other elements. By mass, oxygen is the third most abundant element in the universe after hydrogen and helium and the most abundant element by mass in the Earth's crust, making up almost half of the crust's mass.
Periodic table	The periodic table of the chemical elements (also periodic table of the elements or just the periodic table) is a tabular display of the chemical elements. Although precursors to this table exist, its invention is generally credited to Russian chemist Dmitri Mendeleev in 1869, who intended the table to illustrate recurring ('periodic') trends in the properties of the elements. The layout of the table has been refined and extended over time, as new elements have been discovered, and new theoretical models have been developed to explain chemical behavior.
Permanganate	A permanganate is the general name for a chemical compound containing the manganate(VII) ion, (MnO_4^-). Because manganese is in the +7 oxidation state, the permanganate(VII) ion is a strong oxidizing agent. The ion has tetrahedral geometry.
Calcium	Calcium is the chemical element with the symbol Ca and atomic number 20. It has an atomic mass of 40.078 amu. Calcium is a soft gray alkaline earth metal, and is the fifth most abundant element by mass in the Earth's crust. Calcium is also the fifth most abundant dissolved ion in seawater by both molarity and mass, after sodium, chloride, magnesium, and sulfate.
Calcium hypochlorite	Calcium hypochlorite is a chemical compound with formula $Ca(ClO)_2$. It is widely used for water treatment and as a bleaching agent (bleaching powder). This chemical is considered to be relatively stable and has greater available chlorine than sodium hypochlorite (liquid bleach).
Chlorine	Chlorine (/ˈkl??ri?n/ KLOHR-een; from the Greek word 'χλωρός' (khlôros, meaning 'pale green')) is the chemical element with atomic number 17 and symbol Cl. It is a halogen, found in the periodic table in group 17. As the chloride ion, which is part of common salt and other compounds, it is abundant in nature and necessary to most forms of life, including humans. In its elemental form (Cl_2 or 'dichlorine') under standard conditions, chlorine is a powerful oxidant and is used in bleaching and disinfectants, as well as an essential reagent in the chemical industry.

Chapter 7. SEVEN - OXIDATION - REDUCTION REACTIONS

Sodium	Sodium is a metallic element with a symbol Na and atomic number 11. It is a soft, silvery-white, highly reactive metal and is a member of the alkali metals within 'group 1' (formerly known as 'group IA'). It has only one stable isotope, ^{23}Na.
	Elemental sodium was first isolated by Humphry Davy in 1807 by passing an electric current through molten sodium hydroxide.
Sodium hypochlorite	Sodium hypochlorite is a chemical compound with the formula NaClO. Sodium hypochlorite solution, commonly known as bleach, is frequently used as a disinfectant or a bleaching agent.
	Production
	Hypochlorite was first produced in 1789 by Claude Louis Berthollet in his laboratory on the quay Javel in Paris, France, by passing chlorine gas through a solution of sodium carbonate. The resulting liquid, known as 'Eau de Javel' ('Javel water'), was a weak solution of sodium hypochlorite.
Hypochlorite	The hypochlorite ion, also known as chlorate(I) anion is ClO$^-$. A hypochlorite compound is a chemical compound containing this group, with chlorine in oxidation state +1.
	Hypochlorites are the salts of hypochlorous acid.
Ferrous	Ferrous chemical science, indicates a bivalent iron compound (+2 oxidation state), as opposed to ferric, which indicates a trivalent iron compound (+3 oxidation state).
	Outside of chemical science, ferrous is an adjective used to indicate the presence of iron. Ferrous metals include steel and pig iron (with a carbon content of a few percent) and alloys of iron with other metals (such as stainless steel).

Chapter 7. SEVEN - OXIDATION - REDUCTION REACTIONS

Amorphous carbon	Amorphous carbon, reactive carbon, is an allotrope of carbon that does not have any crystalline structure. As with all glassy materials, some short-range order can be observed. Amorphous carbon is often abbreviated to aC for general amorphous carbon, aC:H for hydrogenated amorphous carbon, or to ta-C for tetrahedral amorphous carbon.
Ammonium	The ammonium cation is a positively charged polyatomic cation with the chemical formula NH_4^+. It is formed by the protonation of ammonia (NH_3). Ammonium is also a general name for positively charged or protonated substituted amines and quaternary ammonium cations (N^+R_4), where one or more hydrogen atoms are replaced by organic radical groups (indicated by R).
Ammonium sulfate	Ammonium sulfate, $(NH_4)_2SO_4$, is an inorganic salt with a number of commercial uses. The most common use is as a soil fertilizer. It contains 21% nitrogen as ammonium cations, and 24% sulfur as sulfate anions.
Reduction potential	Reduction potential (also known as redox potential, oxidation / reduction potential is a measure of the tendency of a chemical species to acquire electrons and thereby be reduced. Reduction potential is measured in volts (V), or millivolts (mV). Each species has its own intrinsic reduction potential; the more positive the potential, the greater the species' affinity for electrons and tendency to be reduced.
Reaction quotient	In chemistry, a reaction quotient: Q_r is a function of the activities or concentrations of the chemical species involved in a chemical reaction. In the special case that the reaction is at equilibrium the reaction quotient is equal to the equilibrium constant. A general chemical reaction in which α moles of a reactant A and β moles of a reactant B react to give σ moles of a product S and τ moles of a product T can be written as αA + βB ⇌ σS + τT The reaction is written as an equilibrium even though in many cases it may appear to have gone to completion.

Chapter 7. SEVEN - OXIDATION - REDUCTION REACTIONS

Dissolution	Dissolution is the process by which a solid or liquid forms a solution in a solvent. In solids this can be explained as the breakdown of the crystal lattice into individual ions, atoms or molecules and their transport into the solvent. Dissolution testing is widely used in the pharmaceutical industry for optimization of formulation and quality control.
Sodium thiosulfate	Sodium thiosulfate is a colorless crystalline compound that is more familiar as the pentahydrate, $Na_2S_2O_3 \cdot 5H_2O$, an efflorescent, monoclinic crystalline substance also called sodium hyposulfite or 'hypo.' The thiosulfate anion is tetrahedral in shape and is notionally derived by replacing one of the oxygen atoms by a sulfur atom in a sulfate anion. The S-S distance indicates a single bond, implying that the sulfur bears significant negative charge and the S-O interactions have more double bond character. The first protonation of thiosulfate occurs at sulfur.
Thiosulfate	Thiosulfate is an oxyanion of sulfur produced by the reaction of sulfite ions with elemental sulfur in boiling water. Thiosulfate occurs naturally in hot springs and geysers, and is produced by certain biochemical processes. It rapidly dechlorinates water, and is notable for its use to halt bleaching in the paper-making industry.
Electrochemical cell	An electrochemical cell is a device capable of either deriving electrical energy from chemical reactions, or facilitating chemical reactions through the introduction of electrical energy. A common example of an electrochemical cell is a standard 1.5-volt 'battery'. (Actually a single 'Galvanic cell'; a battery properly consists of multiple cells).
Ethylenediaminetetraacetic acid	Ethylenediaminetetraacetic acid, widely abbreviated as EDTA is a polyamino carboxylic acid a colourless, water-soluble solid. Its conjugate base is named ethylenediaminetetraacetate. It widely used to dissolve scale.
Galvanic cell	A Galvanic cell, is an electrochemical cell that derives electrical energy from chemical reactions taking place within the cell. It generally consists of two different metals connected by a salt bridge, or individual half-cells separated by a porous membrane. Volta was the inventor of the voltaic pile, the first electrical battery.

Chapter 7. SEVEN - OXIDATION - REDUCTION REACTIONS

Hydrogen	Hydrogen is the chemical element with atomic number 1. It is represented by the symbol H. With an average atomic weight of 1.007 94 u (1.007 825 u for Hydrogen-1), hydrogen is the lightest and most abundant chemical element, constituting roughly 75 % of the Universe's chemical elemental mass. Stars in the main sequence are mainly composed of hydrogen in its plasma state. Naturally occurring elemental hydrogen is relatively rare on Earth.
Electrode	An electrode is an electrical conductor used to make contact with a nonmetallic part of a circuit (e.g. a semiconductor, an electrolyte or a vacuum). The word was coined by the scientist Michael Faraday from the Greek words elektron (meaning amber, from which the word electricity is derived) and hodos, a way.
Equilibrium constant	For a general chemical equilibrium $$\alpha A + \beta B ... \rightleftharpoons \sigma S + \tau T ...$$ the equilibrium constant can be defined by $$K = \frac{\{S\}^\sigma \{T\}^\tau ...}{\{A\}^\alpha \{B\}^\beta ...}$$ where {A} is the activity of the chemical species A, etc. (activity is a dimensionless quantity). It is conventional to put the activities of the products in the numerator and those of the reactants in the denominator.
Standard electrode potential	In electrochemistry, the standard electrode potential, abbreviated E° or E, is the measure of individual potential of a reversible electrode at standard state, which is with solutes at an effective concentration of 1 mol dm^{-3}, and gases at a pressure of 1 atm. The reduction potential is an intensive property. The values are most often tabulated at 25 °C. The basis for an electrochemical cell such as the galvanic cell is always a redox reaction which can be broken down into two half-reactions: oxidation at anode (loss of electron) and reduction at cathode (gain of electron).

Chapter 7. SEVEN - OXIDATION - REDUCTION REACTIONS

Electrode potential	Electrode potential, E, in electrochemistry, according to an IUPAC definition, is the electromotive force of a cell built of two electrodes: • on the left-hand side is the standard hydrogen electrode, and • on the right-hand side is the electrode the potential of which is being defined. By convention: Potential of a cell assembled of two electrodes can be determined from the two individual electrode potentials using: $$\Delta V_{cell} = E_{red,cathode} - E_{red,anode}$$ or, equivalently, $$\Delta V_{cell} = E_{red,cathode} + E_{oxy,anode}$$ This follows from the IUPAC definition of the electric potential difference of a galvanic cell, according to which the electric potential difference of a cell is the difference of the potentials of the electrodes on the right and the left of the galvanic cell. When ΔV_{cell} is positive, then positive electrical charge flows through the cell from the left electrode (anode) to the right electrode (cathode).
Daniell cell	The Daniell cell was invented in 1836 by John Frederic Daniell, a British chemist and meteorologist, and consisted of a copper pot filled with a copper sulphate solution, in which was immersed an unglazed earthenware container filled with sulphuric acid and a zinc electrode.
Activity	In chemical thermodynamics, activity is a measure of the 'effective concentration' of a species in a mixture. By convention, it is treated as a dimensionless quantity, although its actual value depends on customary choices of standard state for the species. The activity of pure substances in condensed phases (solid or liquids) is normally taken as unity.

Chapter 7. SEVEN - OXIDATION - REDUCTION REACTIONS

Corrosion	Corrosion is the disintegration of an engineered material into its constituent atoms due to chemical reactions with its surroundings. In the most common use of the word, this means electrochemical oxidation of metals in reaction with an oxidant such as oxygen. Formation of an oxide of iron due to oxidation of the iron atoms in solid solution is a well-known example of electrochemical corrosion, commonly known as rusting.
Peat	Peat, is an accumulation of partially decayed vegetation matter or histosol. Peat forms in wetland bogs, moors, muskegs, pocosins, mires, and peat swamp forests. Peat is harvested as an important source of fuel in certain parts of the world.
Solubility	Solubility is the property of a solid, liquid, or gaseous chemical substance called solute to dissolve in a liquid solvent to form a homogeneous solution of the solute in the solvent. The solubility of a substance fundamentally depends on the used solvent as well as on temperature and pressure. The extent of the solubility of a substance in a specific solvent is measured as the saturation concentration where adding more solute does not increase the concentration of the solution.
Bromine	Bromine (/ˈbroʊmiːn/ BROH-meen or /ˈbroʊmɪn/ BROH-min; from Greek: βρῶμος, brómos, meaning 'stench (of he-goats)'), is a chemical element with the symbol Br, an atomic number of 35, and an atomic mass of 79.904. It is in the halogen element group. The element was isolated independently by two chemists in 1825-26. Elemental bromine is a fuming red-brown liquid at room temperature, corrosive and toxic, with properties between those of chlorine and iodine. Free bromine does not occur in nature, but occurs as colorless soluble crystalline mineral halide salts, analogous to table salt.
Boltzmann constant	The Boltzmann constant is the physical constant relating energy at the individual particle level with temperature, which must necessarily be observed at the collective or bulk level. It is the gas constant R divided by the Avogadro constant N_A: $$k = \frac{R}{N_A}$$ It has the same units as entropy. he Austrian physicist Ludwig Boltzmann.
Sunlight	

Chapter 7. SEVEN - OXIDATION - REDUCTION REACTIONS

	Sunlight, in the broad sense, is the total frequency spectrum of electromagnetic radiation given off by the Sun. On Earth, sunlight is filtered through the Earth's atmosphere, and solar radiation is obvious as daylight when the Sun is above the horizon.
	When the direct solar radiation is not blocked by clouds, it is experienced as sunshine, a combination of bright light and radiant heat.
Iodine	Iodine is a chemical element that has the symbol I and the atomic number 53.
	Iodine and its compounds are primarily used in nutrition, the production of acetic acid and polymers. Iodine's relatively high atomic number, low toxicity, and ease of attachment to organic compounds have made it a part of many X-ray contrast materials in modern medicine.
Anode	An anode is an electrode through which electric current flows into a polarized electrical device. Mnemonic: ACID (Anode Current Into Device).
	A widespread misconception is that anode polarity is always positive (+).
Cathodic protection	Cathodic protection is a technique used to control the corrosion of a metal surface by making it the cathode of an electrochemical cell. The simplest method to apply cathodic\ protection is by connecting the metal to be protected with another more easily corroded 'sacrificial metal' to act as the anode of the electrochemical cell. Cathodic protection systems are used to protect a wide range of metallic structures in various environments.

Chapter 7. SEVEN - OXIDATION - REDUCTION REACTIONS

Embrittlement	Embrittlement is a loss of ductility of a material, making it brittle. Various materials have different mechanisms of embrittlement. • Hydrogen embrittlement is the effect of hydrogen absorption on some metals and alloys. • Sulfide stress cracking is the embrittlement caused by absorption of hydrogen sulfide. • Liquid metal embrittlement is the embrittlement caused by liquid metals. • Metal-induced embrittlement is the embrittlement caused by diffusion of atoms of metal, either solid or liquid, into the material. • Neutron radiation causes embrittlement of some materials, neutron-induced swelling, and buildup of Wigner energy.
Cathode	A cathode is an electrode through which electric current flows out of a polarized electrical device. Mnemonic: CCD (Cathode Current Departs). A widespread misconception is that cathode polarity is always negative.
Galvanic series	The galvanic series determines the nobility of metals and semi-metals. When two metals are submerged in an electrolyte, while electrically connected, the less noble (base) will experience galvanic corrosion. The rate of corrosion is determined by the electrolyte and the difference in nobility.
Seawater	Seawater is water from a sea or ocean. On average, seawater in the world's oceans has a salinity of about 3.5% (35 g/L, or 599 mM). This means that every kilogram (roughly one litre by volume) of seawater has approximately 35 grams (1.2 oz) of dissolved salts (predominantly Sodium Chloride ions: Na^+, Cl^-).
Atomic number	In chemistry and physics, the atomic number is the number of protons found in the nucleus of an atom and therefore identical to the charge number of the nucleus. It is conventionally represented by the symbol Z. The atomic number uniquely identifies a chemical element. In an atom of neutral charge, the atomic number is also equal to the number of electrons.

Chapter 7. SEVEN - OXIDATION - REDUCTION REACTIONS

Atomic weight	Atomic weight is a dimensionless physical quantity, the ratio of the average mass of atoms of an element (from a given source) to 1/12 of the mass of an atom of carbon-12 (known as the unified atomic mass unit). The term is usually used, without further qualification, to refer to the standard atomic weights published at regular intervals by the International Union of Pure and Applied Chemistry (IUPAC) and which are intended to be applicable to normal laboratory materials.
Concentration	In chemistry, concentration is defined as the abundance of a constituent divided by the total volume of a mixture. Furthermore, in chemistry, four types of mathematical description can be distinguished: mass concentration, molar concentration, number concentration, and volume concentration. The term concentration can be applied to any kind of chemical mixture, but most frequently it refers to solutes in solutions.
Concentration cell	A Concentration cell is an electrochemical cell that has two equivalent half-cells of the same material differing only in concentrations. One can calculate the potential developed by such a cell using the Nernst Equation. A concentration cell produces a voltage as it attempts to reach equilibrium, which will occur when the concentration in both cells are equal.
Intensity	In physics, intensity is a measure of the energy flux, averaged over the period of the wave. The word 'intensity' here is not synonymous with 'strength', 'amplitude', or 'level', as it sometimes is in colloquial speech. For example, 'the intensity of pressure' is meaningless, since the parameters of those variables do not match.
Calcite	Calcite is a carbonate mineral and the most stable polymorph of calcium carbonate ($CaCO_3$). The other polymorphs are the minerals aragonite and vaterite. Aragonite will change to calcite at 470 ° C, and vaterite is even less stable.
Calcium carbonate	Calcium carbonate is a chemical compound with the formula $CaCO_3$. It is a common substance found in rocks in all parts of the world, and is the main component of shells of marine organisms, snails, pearls, and eggshells. Calcium carbonate is the active ingredient in agricultural lime, and is usually the principal cause of hard water.
Passivation	Passivation is the process of making a material 'passive', usually by the deposition of a layer of oxide on its surface. In air, passivation affects the properties of almost all metals-notable examples being aluminium, zinc, titanium, and silicon. In the context of corrosion, passivation is the spontaneous formation of a hard non-reactive surface film that inhibits further corrosion.

Chapter 7. SEVEN - OXIDATION - REDUCTION REACTIONS

Coating	Coating is a covering that is applied to the surface of an object, usually referred to as the substrate. In many cases coatings are applied to improve surface properties of the substrate, such as appearance, adhesion, wetability, corrosion resistance, wear resistance, and scratch resistance. In other cases, in particular in printing processes and semiconductor device fabrication (where the substrate is a wafer), the coating forms an essential part of the finished product.
Material	Material is anything made of matter, constituted of one or more substances. Wood, cement, hydrogen, air and water are all examples of materials. Sometimes the term 'material' is used more narrowly to refer to substances or components with certain physical properties that are used as inputs to production or manufacturing.
Oxide	An oxide is an anion of oxygen in the oxidation state of −2 or a chemical compound formally containing an oxygen in this state. Most of the Earth's crust consists of oxides. Oxides result when elements are oxidized by oxygen in air.
Precipitation	Precipitation is the formation of a solid in a solution or inside another solid during a chemical reaction or by diffusion in a solid. When the reaction occurs in a liquid, the solid formed is called the precipitate, or when compacted by a centrifuge, a pellet. The liquid remaining above the solid is in either case called the supernate or supernatant.
Saturation	In chemistry, saturation has six different meanings, all based on reaching a maximum capacity 1. In physical chemistry, saturation is the point at which a solution of a substance can dissolve no more of that substance and additional amounts of it will appear as a precipitate. This point of maximum concentration, the saturation point, depends on the temperature of the liquid as well as the chemical nature of the substances involved. This can be used in the process of recrystallisation to purify a chemical: it is dissolved to the point of saturation in hot solvent, then as the solvent cools and the solubility decreases, excess solute precipitates.
Deoxygenation	Deoxygenation is a chemical reaction involving the removal of molecular oxygen (O_2) from a reaction mixture or solvent, or the removal of oxygen atoms from a molecule.

Chapter 7. SEVEN - OXIDATION - REDUCTION REACTIONS

Classic representatives of deoxygenation are:

- the replacement of a hydroxyl group by hydrogen (A-OH → A-H) in the Barton-McCombie deoxygenation or in the Markó-Lam deoxygenation
- the replacement of an oxo group by two hydrogen atoms (A=O → A) in the Wolff-Kishner reduction

A chemical reagent for the deoxygenation of many sulfur and nitrogen oxo compounds is the trifluoroacetic anhydride / sodium iodide combination for example in the deoxygenation of the sulfoxide diphenylsulfoxide to the sulfide diphenylsulfide:

The reaction mechanism is based on activation of the sulfoxide by a trifluoroacetyl group and oxidation of iodine. Iodine is formed quantitatively in this reaction and therefore the reagent is used for the analytical detection of many oxo compounds.

Pyrite	The mineral pyrite, is an iron sulfide with the formula FeS_2. This mineral's metallic luster and pale-to-normal, brass-yellow hue have earned it the nickname fool's gold because of its resemblance to gold. The color has also led to the nicknames brass, brazzle and Brazil, primarily used to refer to pyrite found in coal.
Chemical kinetics	Chemical kinetics, is the study of rates of chemical processes. Chemical kinetics includes investigations of how different experimental conditions can influence the speed of a chemical reaction and yield information about the reaction's mechanism and transition states, as well as the construction of mathematical models that can describe the characteristics of a chemical reaction. In 1864, Peter Waage and Cato Guldberg pioneered the development of chemical kinetics by formulating the law of mass action, which states that the speed of a chemical reaction is proportional to the quantity of the reacting substances.
Hypochlorous acid	Hypochlorous acid is a weak acid with the chemical formula HClO. In the swimming pool industry, hypochlorous acid is referred to as HOCl. It forms when chlorine dissolves in water. HClO is an oxidizer, and in its sodium form Sodium hypochlorite, NaClO, or its calcium form Calcium hypochlorite, is used as a bleach, a deodorant, and a disinfectant.
Ammonia	Ammonia is a compound of nitrogen and hydrogen with the formula NH_3. It is a colourless gas with a characteristic pungent odour. Ammonia contributes significantly to the nutritional needs of terrestrial organisms by serving as a precursor to food and fertilizers.

Chapter 7. SEVEN - OXIDATION - REDUCTION REACTIONS

Chloramine	Chloramine is an inorganic compound with the formula NH_2Cl. It is a colourless liquid at room temperature, but it is usually handled as a dilute solution where it is used as a disinfectant. The term chloramine also refers to a family of organic compounds with the formulas R_2NCl and $RNCl_2$ (R is an organic group).
Nitrite	The nitrite ion has the chemical formula NO_2^-. The anion is symmetric with equal N-O bond lengths and a O-N-O bond angle of ca. 120°. On protonation the unstable weak acid nitrous acid is produced.
Polysulfide	Polysulfides are a class of chemical compounds containing chains of sulfur atoms. There are two main classes of polysulfides: anions and organic polysulfides. Anions have the general formula S_n^{2-}.
Hydrazine	Hydrazine is an inorganic chemical compound with the formula N_2H_4. It is a colourless flammable liquid with an ammonia-like odor and is derived from the same industrial chemistry processes that manufacture ammonia. However, hydrazine has physical properties that are closer to those of water.
Hydroxylamine	Hydroxylamine is an inorganic compound with the formula NH_2OH. The pure material is a white, unstable crystalline, hygroscopic compound. However, hydroxylamine is almost always provided and used as an aqueous solution. It is used to prepare oximes, an important functional group.
Nitrogen	Nitrogen is a chemical element that has the symbol N, atomic number of 7 and atomic mass 14.00674 u. Elemental nitrogen is a colorless, odorless, tasteless and mostly inert diatomic gas at standard conditions, constituting 78.08% by volume of Earth's atmosphere. The element nitrogen was discovered as a separable component of air, by Scottish physician Daniel Rutherford, in 1772.
Nitrogen trichloride	Nitrogen trichloride, trichlorine nitride (incorrect in nomenclature of binary compounds; Nitrogen trichloride is a sound name following the rules of systematic nomenclature) is the chemical compound with the formula NCl_3. This yellow, oily, pungent-smelling liquid is most commonly encountered as a byproduct of chemical reactions between ammonia-derivatives and chlorine (for example, in swimming pools between disinfecting chlorine and urea in urine from bathers). In pure form, NCl_3 is highly reactive.

Chapter 7. SEVEN - OXIDATION - REDUCTION REACTIONS

Methylamine	Methylamine is the organic compound with a formula of CH_3NH_2. This colourless gas is a derivative of ammonia, but with one H atom replaced by a methyl group. It is the simplest primary amine.
Phenol	Phenol is an organic compound with the chemical formula C_6H_5OH. It is a white crystalline solid. The molecule consists of a phenyl ($-C_6H_5$), bonded to a hydroxyl (-OH) group. It is produced on a large scale (about 7 billion kg/year) as a precursor to many materials and useful compounds. It is only mildly acidic but requires careful handling due to its propensity to cause burns.
Chloroform	Chloroform is the organic compound with formula $CHCl_3$. The colorless, sweet-smelling, dense liquid is a trihalomethane, and is considered somewhat hazardous. Several million tons are produced annually as a precursor to Teflon and refrigerants, but its use for refrigerants is being phased out.
Trihalomethane	Trihalomethanes (THMs) are chemical compounds in which three of the four hydrogen atoms of methane (CH_4) are replaced by halogen atoms. Many trihalomethanes find uses in industry as solvents or refrigerants. THMs are also environmental pollutants, and many are considered carcinogenic.
Acetone	Acetone is the organic compound with the formula $(CH_3)_2CO$. This colorless, mobile, flammable liquid is the simplest example of the ketones. Acetone is miscible with water and serves as an important solvent in its own right, typically as the solvent of choice for cleaning purposes in the laboratory. About 5.1 million tonnes were produced worldwide in 2009, mainly for use as a solvent and production of methyl methacrylate and bisphenol A. Familiar household uses of acetone are as the active ingredient in nail polish remover and as paint thinner.
Oxalic acid	Oxalic acid is an organic compound with the formula $H_2C_2O_4$. This colourless solid is a dicarboxylic acid. In terms of acid strength, it is about 3,000 times stronger than acetic acid.
Biosynthesis	Biosynthesis is an enzyme-catalyzed process in cells of living organisms by which substrates are converted to more complex products. The biosynthesis process often consists of several enzymatic steps in which the product of one step is used as substrate in the following step. Examples for such multi-step biosynthetic pathways are those for the production of amino acids, fatty acids, and natural products.

Chapter 7. SEVEN - OXIDATION - REDUCTION REACTIONS

Catalysis	Catalysis is the change in rate of a chemical reaction due to the participation of a substance called a catalyst. Unlike other reagents that participate in the chemical reaction, a catalyst is not consumed by the reaction itself. A catalyst may participate in multiple chemical transformations.
Amination	Amination is the process by which an amine group is introduced into an organic molecule. Enzymes which catalyse this reaction, are termed aminases. This can occur in a number of ways including reaction with ammonia or another amine such as an alkylation, reductive amination and the Mannich reaction.
Deamination	Deamination is the removal of an amine group from a molecule. Enzymes which catalyse this reaction are called deaminases. In the human body, deamination takes place primarily in the liver, however glutamate is also deaminated in the kidneys.
Nitrate	The nitrate ion is a polyatomic ion with the molecular formula NO_3^- and a molecular mass of 62.0049 g/mol. Structure It is the conjugate base of nitric acid, consisting of one central nitrogen atom surrounded by three identically-bonded oxygen atoms in a trigonal planar arrangement. The nitrate ion carries a formal charge of -1. This results from a combination formal charge in which each of the three oxygens carries a $-\frac{2}{3}$ charge, whereas the nitrogen carries a +1 charge, all these adding up to formal charge of the polyatomic nitrate ion.
Nitrogen cycle	The nitrogen cycle is the process by which nitrogen is converted between its various chemical forms. This transformation can be carried out via both biological and non-biological processes. Important processes in the nitrogen cycle include fixation, mineralization, nitrification, and denitrification.

Chapter 7. SEVEN - OXIDATION - REDUCTION REACTIONS

Fixation	Fixation in alchemy refers to a process by which a previously volatile substance is 'transformed' into a form (often solid) that is not affected by fire. It separates the substance or object and puts it back in the same or different shape at a subatomic level.
	It is one of the 12 vital alchemical processes that are required for transformation of a substance.
Rhizobium	Rhizobium is a genus of Gram-negative soil bacteria that fix nitrogen. Rhizobium forms an endosymbiotic nitrogen fixing association with roots of legumes and Parasponia.
	The bacteria colonize plant cells within root nodules; here the bacteria convert atmospheric nitrogen to ammonia and then provide organic nitrogenous compounds such as glutamine or ureides to the plant.
Acceptor	In semiconductor physics, an acceptor is a dopant atom that when added to a semiconductor can form p-type regions.
	For example, when silicon (Si), having four valence electrons, needs to be doped as a p-type semiconductor, elements from group III like boron (B) or aluminium (Al), having three valence electrons, can be used. The latter elements are also called trivalent impurities.
Electron acceptor	An electron acceptor is a chemical entity that accepts electrons transferred to it from another compound. It is an oxidizing agent that, by virtue of its accepting electrons, is itself reduced in the process.
	Typical oxidizing agents undergo permanent chemical alteration through covalent or ionic reaction chemistry, resulting in the complete and irreversible transfer of one or more electrons.

Chapter 7. SEVEN - OXIDATION - REDUCTION REACTIONS

Formaldehyde

Formaldehyde is an organic compound with the formula CH_2O. It is the simplest aldehyde, hence its systematic name methanal.

Formaldehyde is a colorless gas with a characteristic pungent odor. It is an important precursor to many other chemical compounds, especially for polymers. In 2005, annual world production of formaldehyde was estimated to be 23 million tonnes (50 billion pounds). Commercial solutions of formaldehyde in water, commonly called formalin, were formerly used as disinfectants and for preservation of biological specimens.

Activated sludge

Activated sludge is a process for treating sewage and industrial wastewaters using air and a biological floc composed of bacteria and protozoans.

Purpose
In a sewage (or industrial wastewater) treatment plant, the activated sludge process can be used for one or several of the following purposes:

- oxidizing carbonaceous matter: biological matter.
- oxidizing nitrogeneous matter: mainly ammonium and nitrogen in biological materials.
- removing phosphate.
- driving off entrained gases carbon dioxide, ammonia, nitrogen, etc.
- generating a biological floc that is easy to settle.
- generating a liquor that is low in dissolved or suspended material.

The process
The process involves air or oxygen being introduced into a mixture of primary treated or screened sewage or industrial wastewater (called wastewater from now on) combined with organisms to develop a biological floc which reduces the organic content of the sewage. This material, which in healthy sludge is a brown floc, is largely composed of saprotrophic bacteria but also has an important protozoan flora mainly composed of amoebae, Spirotrichs, Peritrichs including Vorticellids and a range of other filter feeding species.

Chapter 7. SEVEN - OXIDATION - REDUCTION REACTIONS

Fermentation	Fermentation is the process of deriving energy from the oxidation of organic compounds, such as carbohydrates, and using an endogenous electron acceptor, which is usually an organic compound. In contrast, respiration is where electrons are donated to an exogenous electron acceptor, such as oxygen, via an electron transport chain. Fermentation is important in anaerobic conditions when there is no oxidative phosphorylation to maintain the production of ATP (Adenosine triphosphate) by glycolysis.
Methane	Methane is a chemical compound with the chemical formula CH_4. It is the simplest alkane, and the principal component of natural gas. Methane's bond angles are 109.5 degrees.
Sludge	Sludge refers to the residual, semi-solid material left from industrial wastewater, or sewage treatment processes. It can also refer to the settled suspension obtained from conventional drinking water treatment, and numerous other industrial processes. The term is also sometimes used as a generic term for solids separated from suspension in a liquid; this 'soupy' material usually contains significant quantities of 'interstitial' water (between the solid particles).
Carbon	Carbon is the chemical element with symbol C and atomic number 6. As a member of group 14 on the periodic table, it is nonmetallic and tetravalent--making four electrons available to form covalent chemical bonds. There are three naturally occurring isotopes, with ^{12}C and ^{13}C being stable, while ^{14}C is radioactive, decaying with a half-life of about 5730 years. Carbon is one of the few elements known since antiquity.
Adsorption	Adsorption is the adhesion of atoms, ions, biomolecules or molecules of gas, liquid, or dissolved solids to a surface. This process creates a film of the adsorbate (the molecules or atoms being accumulated) on the surface of the adsorbent. It differs from absorption, in which a fluid permeates or is dissolved by a liquid or solid.
Anaerobic digestion	Anaerobic digestion is a series of processes in which microorganisms break down biodegradable material in the absence of oxygen, used for industrial or domestic purposes to manage waste and/or to release energy. It is widely used as part of the process to treat wastewater. As part of an integrated waste management system, anaerobic digestion reduces the emission of landfill gas into the atmosphere.

Chapter 7. SEVEN - OXIDATION - REDUCTION REACTIONS

Digestion	In alchemy, Digestion is a process in which gentle heat is applied to a substance over a period of several weeks. This was traditionally performed by sealing a sample of the substance in a flask, and keeping the flask in fresh horse dung or sometimes in direct sunlight. Today, practitioners of alchemy use thermostat-controlled incubators.
Liquid	Liquid is one of the three classical states of matter. Like a gas, a liquid is able to flow and take the shape of a container. Some liquids resist compression, while others can be compressed.
Reference electrode	A Reference electrode is an electrode which has a stable and well-known electrode potential. The high stability of the electrode potential is usually reached by employing a redox system with constant (buffered or saturated) concentrations of each participants of the redox reaction. There are many ways reference electrodes are used.
Sodium chloride	Sodium chloride, common salt, table salt, or halite, is an ionic compound with the formula NaCl. Sodium chloride is the salt most responsible for the salinity of the ocean and of the extracellular fluid of many multicellular organisms. As the major ingredient in edible salt, it is commonly used as a condiment and food preservative.
Salt bridge	A salt bridge, in chemistry, is a laboratory device used to connect the oxidation and reduction half-cells of a galvanic cell (voltaic cell), a type of electrochemical cell. Salt bridges usually come in two types: glass tube and filter paper. The conductivity of a glass tube bridge depends mostly on the concentration of the electrolyte solution.

Chapter 7. SEVEN - OXIDATION - REDUCTION REACTIONS

Saturated calomel electrode	The Saturated calomel electrode is a reference electrode based on the reaction between elemental mercury and mercury(I) chloride. The aqueous phase in contact with the mercury and the mercury(I) chloride (Hg_2Cl_2, 'calomel') is a saturated solution of potassium chloride in water. The electrode is normally linked via a porous frit to the solution in which the other electrode is immersed.
Silver chloride electrode	A silver chloride electrode is a type of reference electrode, commonly used in electrochemical measurements. For example, it is usually the internal reference electrode in pH meters. As another example, the silver chloride electrode is the most commonly used reference electrode for testing cathodic protection corrosion control systems in sea water environments.
Glass electrode	A glass electrode is a type of ion-selective electrode made of a doped glass membrane that is sensitive to a specific ion. It is an important part of the instrumentation for chemical analysis and physico-chemical studies. In modern practice, widely used membranous ion-selective electrodes (ISE, including glasses) are part of a galvanic cell.
PH meter	A pH meter is an electronic instrument used for measuring the pH (acidity or alkalinity) of a liquid (though special probes are sometimes used to measure the pH of semi-solid substances). A typical pH meter consists of a special measuring probe (a glass electrode) connected to an electronic meter that measures and displays the pH reading. The probe The pH probe measures pH as the activity of hydrogen cations surrounding a thin-walled glass bulb at its tip.
Divalent	In chemistry, a divalent ion or molecule has a valence of two and thus can form two covalent bonds with other ions or molecules. An older term for divalent is bivalent. Divalent anions are atoms or radicals with two additional electrons when compared to their elemental state (that is, with 2 more electrons than protons).
Polarization	Polarization in corrosion refers to any changes in the equilibrium potential of an electrochemical reaction.

Chapter 7. SEVEN - OXIDATION - REDUCTION REACTIONS

Dropping mercury electrode	The dropping mercury electrode is a working electrode made of mercury and used in polarography. Experiments run with mercury electrodes are referred to as forms of polarography even if the experiments are identical or very similar to a corresponding voltammetry experiment which use solid working electrodes. Like other working electrodes these electrodes are used in electrochemical studies using three electrode systems when investigating reaction mechanisms related to redox chemistry among other chemical phenomena.
Absorption	In physics, absorption of electromagnetic radiation is the way by which the energy of a photon is taken up by matter, typically the electrons of an atom. Thus, the electromagnetic energy is transformed to other forms of energy for example, to heat. The absorption of light during wave propagation is often called attenuation.
Mercury	Mercury (/'m?rkj?ri/ or /'m?rk?ri/ MER-k(y)?-ree), also known as quicksilver or hydrargyrum, is a chemical element with the symbol Hg and atomic number 80. Mercury is the only metal that is liquid at standard conditions for temperature and pressure; the only other element that is liquid under these conditions is bromine. With a freezing point of −38.83 °C and boiling point of 356.73 °C, mercury has one of the broadest ranges of its liquid state of any metal. A heavy, silvery d-block metal, mercury is also one of the five metallic chemical elements that are liquid at or near room temperature and pressure, the others being caesium, francium, gallium, and rubidium.
Spectrophotometry	In chemistry, spectrophotometry is the quantitative measurement of the reflection or transmission properties of a material as a function of wavelength. It is more specific than the general term electromagnetic spectroscopy in that spectrophotometry deals with visible light, near-ultraviolet, and near-infrared, but does not cover time-resolved spectroscopic techniques. Spectrophotometry involves the use of a spectrophotometer.
Amperometric titration	Amperometric titration refers to a class of titrations in which the equivalence point is determined through measurement of the electric current produced by the titration reaction. It is a form of quantitative analysis. Background Consider a solution containing the analyte, A, in the presence of some conductive buffer.

Chapter 7. SEVEN - OXIDATION - REDUCTION REACTIONS

Titration	Titration, is a common laboratory method of quantitative chemical analysis that is used to determine the unknown concentration of an identified analyte. Because volume measurements play a key role in titration, it is also known as volumetric analysis. A reagent, called the titrant or titrator is prepared as a standard solution.
Ionization	Ionization is the process of converting an atom or molecule into an ion by adding or removing charged particles such as electrons or other ions. This is often confused with dissociation. A substance may dissociate without necessarily producing ions.
Product	Product(s) are formed during chemical reactions as reagents are consumed. Products have lower energy than the reagents and are produced during the reaction according to the second law of thermodynamics. The released energy comes from changes in chemical bonds between atoms in reagent molecules and may be given off in the form of heat or light.

PRACTICE QUIZ
Chapter 7. SEVEN - OXIDATION - REDUCTION REACTIONS

1. _____ is a compound of nitrogen and hydrogen with the formula NH_3. It is a colourless gas with a characteristic pungent odour. _____ contributes significantly to the nutritional needs of terrestrial organisms by serving as a precursor to food and fertilizers.

    a. Ammonia
    b. Sulfuric acid
    c. Air conditioning
    d. Catalysis

2. _____ is the property of a solid, liquid, or gaseous chemical substance called solute to dissolve in a liquid solvent to form a homogeneous solution of the solute in the solvent. The _____ of a substance fundamentally depends on the used solvent as well as on temperature and pressure. The extent of the _____ of a substance in a specific solvent is measured as the saturation concentration where adding more solute does not increase the concentration of the solution.

    a. 1,2-Dioxetane
    b. 1,3,5-Trioxane
    c. Chloranilic acid
    d. Solubility

3. _____ (/ˈkl??ri?n/ KLOHR-een; from the Greek word 'χλωρός' (khlôros, meaning 'pale green')) is the chemical element with atomic number 17 and symbol Cl. It is a halogen, found in the periodic table in group 17. As the chloride ion, which is part of common salt and other compounds, it is abundant in nature and necessary to most forms of life, including humans. In its elemental form (Cl_2 or 'dichlorine') under standard conditions, _____ is a powerful oxidant and is used in bleaching and disinfectants, as well as an essential reagent in the chemical industry.

    a. Chlorine
    b. Iodine
    c. Oxygen
    d. Ammonium nitrate

4. The _____ is a reference electrode based on the reaction between elemental mercury and mercury(I) chloride. The aqueous phase in contact with the mercury and the mercury(I) chloride (Hg_2Cl_2, 'calomel') is a saturated solution of potassium chloride in water. The electrode is normally linked via a porous frit to the solution in which the other electrode is immersed.

----

a. Silver chloride electrode
b. Saturated calomel electrode
c. Unimolecular rectifier
d. Voltammetry

5. _____ is a loss of ductility of a material, making it brittle. Various materials have different mechanisms of _____.

- Hydrogen _____ is the effect of hydrogen absorption on some metals and alloys.

- Sulfide stress cracking is the _____ caused by absorption of hydrogen sulfide.

- Liquid metal _____ is the _____ caused by liquid metals.

- Metal-induced _____ is the _____ caused by diffusion of atoms of metal, either solid or liquid, into the material.

- Neutron radiation causes _____ of some materials, neutron-induced swelling, and buildup of Wigner energy.

a. Embrittlement
b. Ablation
c. Embedment
d. Ozone cracking

ANSWER KEY
Chapter 7. SEVEN - OXIDATION - REDUCTION REACTIONS

1. a
2. d
3. a
4. b
5. a

You can take the complete Chapter Practice Test

for Chapter 7. SEVEN - OXIDATION - REDUCTION REACTIONS
on all key terms, persons, places, and concepts.

Online 99 Cents

http://www.epub14.6.2184.7.cram101.com/

Use www.Cram101.com for all your study needs

including Cram101's online interactive problem solving labs in chemistry, statistics, mathematics, and more.

Other Cram101 e-Books and Tests

Want More?
Cram101.com...

Cram101.com provides the outlines and highlights of your textbooks, just like this e-StudyGuide, but also gives you the **PRACTICE TESTS**, and other exclusive study tools for all of your textbooks.

Learn More. *Just click*
http://www.cram101.com/

Other Cram101 e-Books and Tests